GHOSTS
AND THE PARANORMAL

❖ Blood-curdling stories from the other side ❖

igloobooks

igloobooks

Published in 2018
by Igloo Books Ltd
Cottage Farm
Sywell
NN6 0BJ
www.igloobooks.com

Copyright © 2018 Igloo Books Ltd

GOL002 1118
2 4 6 8 10 9 7 5 3
ISBN 978-1-78670-486-3

Cover images: Front cover: tl Trigger Image/Alamy Stock Photo;
tc Nikki Ruttley/Alamy Stock Photo; bc Julie S Woodhouse/Alamy Stock Photo
All other imagery: © iStock / Getty Images

Designed by Charlie Wood-Penn
Edited by Bobby Newlyn-Jones

Printed and manufactured in China

CONTENTS

ABOVE Some believe that the human soul leaves the body at the point of death, to continue its journey

GHOSTS AND THE PARANORMAL

Ever since humans first walked on Earth, we have wondered what happens to us after we die. Down the centuries, countless civilisations have imagined that something of us survives after we leave this physical world; that sometimes echoes of the departed remain, or return, to communicate with those they have left behind.

So what, then, is a ghost? Some people believe that we are fundamentally spiritual beings who live our lives for a short while in a physical body. Once that body dies, our spirit survives. Others call this entity our soul. In 1901, one doctor even tried to quantify what this elusive essence might be. Dr Duncan MacDougall measured the weight of six terminally ill patients both before and immediately after their death. All of them weighed less on the instant they died, with an average loss of 21 g (0.7 oz). Was this the weight of their soul? While this scientific approach may seem faintly ridiculous, the number of ghostly and paranormal experiences that people have recorded through history suggests that somehow, sometimes, those who have passed over to the 'other side' either wish to, or cannot help but, communicate with the living.

The great variety of the supernatural experiences recorded shows that ghosts are certainly not a single, specific phenomenon. They cover a wide range of paranormal activities, as this book will show. One possible explanation for this cornucopia of bizarre events is the Stone Tape Theory. This suggests that we are all embodiments of energy and that as we have experiences through our lives, we leave traces of this energy around us. If we have an intensely powerful experience, a trauma or a tragedy, the energy emitted by this leaves an imprint on our surroundings. So, the stones of a castle's walls may be imprinted by the murder of one of its inhabitants, for example. The energy record of these events remains, therefore, and that energy can be picked up by others, in later years, who are sensitive enough to detect it. Could this explain why people report seeing a ghost performing the same action over and over again, such as walking through a wall or slamming a door? Their actions could be the imprinted energy record of an action they performed while they were alive and in a heightened emotional state.

Of course, we cannot know, but we can relish the thrilling diversity and chilling strangeness of these paranormal events.

✝✝✝✝

RIGHT Could a traumatic event leave behind a ghostly imprint?

HAUNTED LOCATIONS

Wherever human beings have lived and died, there is the possibility of seeing a ghost – a spirit unable to make a clean break between this world and the 'other side'. Some haunted locations are private homes, others are open spaces, but wherever we go we might not be alone.

Hotels are special places, providing a home away from home, where we can be pampered a little, perhaps, and have a break from everyday reality. We hope to receive a warm welcome and to be made to feel important. Some hotels, however, seem to harbour some extra, less welcome guests. One of the oldest and most famous hotels in Canada is the Empress Hotel in Victoria, British Columbia. It has hosted royalty and celebrities, but it also has the dubious honour of being one of the most haunted buildings in the country. At the turn of the 20th century, the hotel's architect was Francis Rattenbury and it seems he cannot quite leave his creation. A thin man with a moustache, in an Edwardian suit and with a cane, has often been seen walking the halls. On the sixth floor, a maid appears from nowhere, cleaning and cleaning until she vanishes into thin air. She is sometimes joined by an elderly lady who knocks politely on the doors of guests. If you answer, she may lead you to the elevators where she, too, vanishes.

Still in North America, but down in Manhattan, New York, the Chelsea Hotel has always been one of the hippest, coolest places to stay. An extra chill is added, however, by the hotel's celebrity ghosts. Throughout the 20th century, the Chelsea attracted artists of every kind; writers, musicians and painters. Many of them moved in and lived there permanently, for months or even years. Arthur C Clarke wrote *2001: A Space Odyssey* while living there and Bob Dylan, Andy Warhol and Jimi Hendrix all lived there for a time. Just before his death, the poet Dylan Thomas stayed there, in room 206, and one later guest in that room woke to see him staring at her. So much creative, troubled energy has left its mark on this hotel.

LEFT
The Empress Hotel in Victoria, British Colombia, is said to be one of Canada's most haunted buildings

Another death took place at the Chelsea, in 1978, in room 100. Sid Vicious of the Sex Pistols was living there with his girlfriend, Nancy Spungen. After a night of intense drug-taking, Nancy was found stabbed to death. Sid couldn't remember if he had done it, but later overdosed on heroin to avoid going to prison. Ever since then, guests have reported strange happenings around room 100. Loud music erupts with no source, lights flash and the temperature suddenly plummets. Some have heard the sound of a heated argument coming from the room – when it is empty.

Read on to discover the sinister happenings across the world in homes, castles and palaces, on mountainsides, in forests and at sea. Is nowhere beyond the reach of the undead?

✝✝✝✝

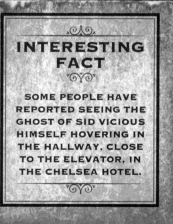

INTERESTING FACT

SOME PEOPLE HAVE REPORTED SEEING THE GHOST OF SID VICIOUS HIMSELF HOVERING IN THE HALLWAY, CLOSE TO THE ELEVATOR, IN THE CHELSEA HOTEL.

ABOVE Some of the celebrities who stayed at New York's Chelsea Hotel may have left behind more than their reputation

ABOVE Sometimes the grave might not be the last
resting place of the departed
INSET Abandoned homes leave behind the secrets
of their former inhabitants

PRIVATE HOMES

Our home should be a place of refuge, the safe place we can retreat to for rest, for joy and for peace. So, when a home becomes the focus for paranormal activity, it can be truly terrifying.

In the 1830s, the Proctor family moved into a mill house in the village of Willington, in Cheshire. Joseph Proctor was a devout Christian, fervently opposed to ideas of the supernatural. One night, as the maid was putting the children to bed, she heard footsteps from the floor above. Reporting the noise to Joseph Proctor, he assured her that such sounds were to be expected in an old house. The following night the footsteps came again. Her master agreed to investigate and found a room that was locked shut, its window boarded up. The dust on the floor showed that no-one had walked across it for a very long time.

The same footsteps were heard by the whole family in the coming months, but they were determined to take no notice. When Mrs Proctor's sisters came to visit, however, the strange activity reached crisis level. The bed they slept in shook uncontrollably across the floor and the curtains opened and closed. As they lay rigid with fright, the spectre of a woman emerged from one wall and leaned over the bed. Joseph then called in an 'expert', a Dr Drury, who although a sceptic was interested in these phenomena. By the time he left the house he was a sceptic no longer.

Modern times can produce stories every bit as unnerving as this one, too. In the 1980s, a couple moved into a lovely house in a new development in Newport, Texas. Soon the lighting and other electronics started behaving erratically. When a series of rectangular holes began to emerge in a pattern on the lawn, they were worried. Contractors next door unearthed a pair of rotting coffins and so it emerged that the whole development was built on the site of a cemetery.

A barrage of haunting forced the neighbours to move out, but this couple were determined to stay and excavate their own garden. When their daughter joined in the task, she suddenly keeled over and died. Needless to say, the couple gave up their struggle and left the neighbourhood without delay.

Over the following pages, we will delve deeper into the horrors that go on behind locked doors in the infamous private homes of Amityville and 50 Berkeley Square, the classic English manor house at Hinton Ampner and the New York brownstone 14 West 10th Street.

50 BERKELEY SQUARE, LONDON, UK

Berkeley Square in London's Mayfair is one of the capital's smartest addresses. Yet one of the houses in this beautiful square has the unenviable reputation of the being the most haunted house in London.

In the early 19th century, 50 Berkeley Square was the home of British Prime Minister George Canning. Later, in the mid-19th century, a Mr Myers moved in and happily prepared the house to receive his bride after their wedding, but she jilted him at the last minute.

Heartbroken, Myers retreated to the top floor of the house, where he lived the life of a recluse in a tiny attic room. He never went out and only opened the front door to receive food from one servant. At night, however, he wandered the house with a single candle. Passers-by in the street were terrified to see this pale light flickering through the decaying mansion – and so the stories began.

A popular magazine, *Mayfair*, wrote about this scary place:

'If there be physiognomy in bricks and mortar, one would say that house has seen murder done ... a valuable house left seemingly to decay, with windows caked and blackened by dust, full of silence and emptiness.'

After Myers died, the terrifying stories about the house began to multiply.

A Lord Lyttleton offered to spend the night in the supposedly haunted attic room, with two hunting guns. On seeing a ghostly apparition he fired one of them, but in the morning only a bullet hole remained. A man then moved in with his two daughters. When the fiancé of one of the girls, a Captain Kentfield, was coming to stay, a maid went to prepare his attic room. Her terrified screams rang through the house and she was found muttering, 'Don't let it touch me.' The stricken maid never recovered and died the next day.

LEFT
Today, 50 Berkeley Square looks like any other smart residence in London's Mayfair

Foolishly, Captain Kentfield offered to spend the night there anyway, but whatever lurked in that attic was not about to leave. He too filled the house with his terrible screams and was found dead on the floor the next morning, his face contorted in a grimace of horror.

What was this ghost? So far, no one had lived to describe it. Was it Myers? Some later sightings said it was a sobbing child, tortured to death in her nursery. Others described the ghost of a woman hanging from a top floor window before she fell to her death, fleeing from an abusive uncle. In the 1880s, two sailors broke into the empty house to sleep. By morning, one was dead and the other had fled in terror.

For most of the 20th century, the ground floor was occupied by an antiquarian bookseller, Maggs Brothers. Staff claimed to hear strange noises upstairs – but they never dared to look. A police notice on the ground floor strictly forbids anyone from venturing upstairs, for any reason whatsoever.

†‡†‡†‡

RIGHT A photo of the front door of 50 Berkeley Square, taken in 1910. Was the photographer brave enough to venture inside?

AMITYVILLE, LONG ISLAND, USA

It may be a private home, but this house at 112 Ocean Avenue, Amityville, Long Island, New York has been very much in the public eye for more than 40 years. It's the setting for one of the scariest stories of haunting and horror the US has ever seen.

On the 13th November 1974, this large, colonial style residence was home to the DeFeo family. It was called, ironically, High Hopes. On that terrible day, Ronald DeFeo Jr shot dead his parents and four siblings in a massacre that shocked the nation. He was soon jailed and the house was sold. Understandably, no buyer came forwards for a while, until in December 1975, George and Kathy Lutz and their three children moved in.

No sooner had they crossed the threshold than the most bizarre and terrifying things started happening. For the next 28 days, the Lutz family were subjected to the most horrific ordeal by a series of unseen forces. First was the plague of flies that young Daniel Lutz found in his new playroom. He swatted as many as he could, then ran screaming to his mother for help, but on their return to the room, every single fly had disappeared. Then objects began flying across rooms and the children would wake up sleeping on their stomachs, in the poses of the dead DeFeos.

Kathy suffered strange injuries and nightmarish visions of the murders, which even told her exactly where each one had taken place. George would wake repeatedly at 3.15 am – although he did not know it, this was precisely the hour of the gruesome murders.

One night, George went to the bottom of the garden to investigate a noise. Looking back at the house, he saw a chilling sight – a pair of blood-red eyes shining out from his young daughter Missy's bedroom window. Rushing back inside to her, he found her fast asleep, but she did later talk of her 'new friend', a pig-like creature whose eyes, she said, glowed red.

LEFT
The Amityville Horror movie poster from 1979

ABOVE The Amityville Horror house, taken in 2006

Then there was the Red Room, a mysterious room in the basement that was not on the house plans, but that drove the Lutz dog completely wild with fear. Realising something was badly wrong, the family summoned a priest to carry out a blessing on the house. Only later did he confess that, as he recited a prayer, he heard the words, 'Will you stop!' and felt a slap on his hands.

Finally, the Lutz family could stand it no longer. They fled the house and never returned. Their story became a novel and then a hit movie, *The Amityville Horror*, in 1979. Many people have challenged their tale, suggesting it was a giant hoax cooked up for money, but George and Kathy insisted it was genuine until their deaths many years later – and they both passed a lie detector test.

INTERESTING FACT

112 OCEAN AVENUE IS NOW 108 OCEAN AVENUE. A PREVIOUS OWNER ASKED THE POSTAL SERVICE TO HAVE IT CHANGED.

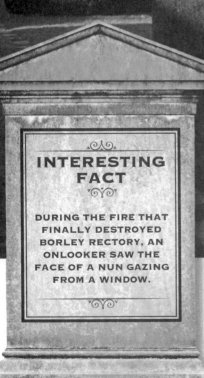

ABOVE Borley Rectory stood beside the village's pretty country church and churchyard. The church has also laid claims to ghostly goings-on, but nothing compared to its neighbour

INSET In 1955, a little girl peers down the path in the garden of the abandoned Rectory, where a nun has frequently been seen, searching for her lover

BORLEY RECTORY, ESSEX, UK

There is something about rectories and their long histories that make them intriguing buildings. This one in East England takes the prize as the creepiest of them all and for a long time it enjoyed the chilling distinction of being called the most haunted house in England.

The small village of Borley lies just on the Essex side of the Essex-Suffolk border. The rectory was built back in 1863, but centuries earlier there had been a monastery on that site and it was there that the troubles began. One of the monks is said to have fallen in love with a nun from the local nunnery. They planned to run away, abandoning their religious vows, but they were caught. The penalty for their love was death and a grim one at that. The monk was hanged in the monastery, while the nun was sealed up alive in its walls. In the 19th century, she was seen many times, walking desperately through the grounds of the rectory, searching for her lover.

The spectral appearances became much more threatening after the death of the first rector, Reverend Harry Bull. His children fled the house after seeing a ghostly horse-drawn carriage chasing the nun across the garden, but for the Reverend Eric Smith, who moved in next, there was worse to come. In 1928, he contacted a national newspaper to report mysterious footsteps, doorbells ringing of their own accord and other unexplained sounds. The newspaper sent in Harry Price, a paranormal investigator. On his very first night, he saw a spectral figure in the garden and then, suddenly, a pane of glass crashed out of a porch window and smashed to the ground. As he went inside, a red vase from an upstairs sitting room flew past him down the stairs and smashed in the hall. Reverend Smith tried to exorcise the property, but the unquiet spirits refused to leave, so he and his wife eventually left the house for good.

The Foysters were the next inhabitants. They suffered five years of the same violent torment. One terrible night, Mrs Foyster was even thrown out of her bed by an unseen force. When they could stand no more, they left. Harry Price moved back in. In 1938, he held a séance to contact the spirit. A message tapped on the walls said the house would burn to the ground that night. Next morning the rectory still stood, but a year later a lamp overturned and a devastating fire destroyed the whole house.

MONTE CRISTO HOMESTEAD, AUSTRALIA

Stories of hauntings and horror are to be found in all corners of the world. In New South Wales, Australia, one house in the town of Junee has a very dark history indeed. So dark that it is widely accepted as the most haunted house in Australia, one that has chilled even the most hardened of ghost-hunters.

Junee is a small town, not at all out of the ordinary - except that one of its homes, Monte Cristo, has some terrible tales to tell, including murder, torture and suicide. The elegant two-storey house, built in 1884, looks from the outside like a dream home. Yet ever since its first residents - the Crawley family - moved in, one tragedy has followed another. First, their young baby daughter died after being dropped by her nanny down the stairs. This was no ordinary accident. The nanny claimed that an unseen force pushed the baby out of her arms. Today, young children visiting the house often become very agitated and scared around that staircase, as if a dying child is reaching out to them.

As if that wasn't tragic enough, when one of the Crawleys' maids became pregnant, she was so desperate that she jumped to her death from the balcony that runs along the front of the house. A ghostly apparition of a young woman in 19th century clothes has often been seen gliding along this balcony and although the bloodstained steps below have been scrubbed over and over again, the stain cannot be removed.

The third ghostly figure to appear at Monte Cristo is that of a young boy, a stable hand named Morris. He would sleep in the stables, but one day he was too ill to get up for work. Believing he was faking illness, his boss set fire to his bedding. Poor Morris was not faking it and he could not get up. He was burned alive where he lay. The ghost of this tormented soul has often been seen by the coach house.

Mrs Crawley died in the house in 1933. She, too, is often seen patrolling her old home. She seems to take against some of the guests who visit the house and makes her feelings known. Chillingly, she has been known to order people out of the dining room or the chapel – and after her appearance they are all too ready to leave.

The Ryan family moved in, in 1963, and live there still. Mr Ryan is surprisingly comfortable with his home's extra guests and opens Monte Cristo to visitors. They are invited to spend the night in the house – but most do not last the night. Feelings of misery and dread overwhelm them, they hear footsteps and see visions and they flee this place of tormented souls.

INSET One tragedy after another befell the residents of the Monte Cristo Homestead

RIGHT Young Morris' screams are said to resonate around the stables where he died in the fire

> Courage is resistance to fear, mastery of fear, not absence of fear.
>
> Mark Twain

HOUSE OF DEATH, NEW YORK

New York is a dynamic, fast-paced city, not the kind of place you associate with hauntings and the paranormal. Yet in this 'city that never sleeps', it seems the spirits of some of its past residents cannot find rest.

The house at 14 West 10th Street is the last 'unresting' place of an extraordinary, and chilling, 22 ghosts. This impressive house, now known as the House of Death, is a classic New York brownstone, built in the 1850s in lower Manhattan. It was home to many of the city's elite, until in 1900, a novelist moved in called Samuel Clemens. He was better known by his writing name, Mark Twain. Although he only stayed for a year, he certainly left his mark on the house. His restless spirit has been seen wandering through the first floor in a white suit. In the 1930s, a mother and daughter said they saw him sitting by a window where he told them, 'My name is Clemens and I has a problem here I gotta settle,' before he vanished into thin air.

There are more unsettled spirits here. Ghost hunters and investigators galore have visited the house, and many have sensed the presence of a ghostly lady in white, as well as a grey cat. Who knows what sorrowful stories these spirits would have to tell if they could speak to us?

Sadly, we know too well the story behind the ghost of a young girl that haunts this creepy house. The house was converted into apartments in the 1930s, and in 1987 a lawyer named Joel Steinberg was living in one of them on the second floor. With him was his 6-year-old, illegally adopted daughter, Lisa, and a baby. One November night, the police received a call from the apartment about a child who was not breathing. When they broke in, they found Lisa unconscious, and the baby covered in filth and chained to a playpen. The baby survived this terrible treatment, but Lisa tragically died. Joel Steinberg was imprisoned, but it seems poor Lisa has never been quite able to leave the scene of the crime.

†┼╪┼†

INSET Mark Twain pictured in 1907 wearing the white suit he has been spotted in. It appears that he, and others, have been unable to leave this brownstone house in New York

RIGHT The gloomy 14 West 10th Street in the Greenwich Village neighbourhood of Manhattan, New York City

ABOVE The previous house used to stand where the lawns of Hinton Ampner are today. The troubled site was home to some chilling tales

HINTON AMPNER, UK

The classic English manor house at Hinton Ampner in Hampshire is today looked after by the National Trust. On summer afternoons, the house and its beautiful gardens are full of carefree visitors, however just 50 m (165 ft) away, buried beneath the lawns, lie the remains of another manor house.

The original Tudor house was not a happy place. It dates from the 16th century and for hundreds of years it was the scene of a succession of terrifying hauntings, with slamming doors, raised voices, the rustle of silk clothing and heavy footsteps in the night. This was all too much for its petrified residents and eventually the house was demolished in 1793. The haunting of this place is considered one of the greatest English ghost stories and some think it was the tales from Hinton Ampner that inspired the great novelist Henry James to write his terrifying story *The Turn of the Screw* in 1898. But what exactly happened at Hinton Ampner to cause so much spiritual chaos?

In the mid-18th century, the master of the house was Edward, Lord Stawell. He was an 'evil liver' – a bad sort whose cruelty affected all around him. His wife, Mary, died in 1740, but not before Edward had taken up with her beautiful younger sister, Honoria. Locals said the pair had a child together, but the infant disappeared soon after it was born. Honoria died in 1754 and a year later Lord Stawell died mysteriously in the parlour of the house.

Then the sightings began of a gentlemanly figure, plainly dressed just as Lord Stawell had been, standing in the moonlight beside the house. Strange sounds echoed around the house and few servants could bear to stay for more than a few days or weeks.

In 1764, a new family moved in – the Ricketts. No sooner had they arrived than the hauntings multiplied, with doors slamming and footsteps echoing through the house. One night when her husband was away, Mrs Ricketts heard a man's footsteps approach her bed in the dark and a high-pitched female voice in murmured conversation with two men. When she heard something heavy fall over in the next room, she became truly frightened and summoned her brother and a friend to investigate. As they settled down with pistols to watch and wait, a series of terrible groans came from upstairs and one man felt something flit past him. They went to search but found nothing. Terrified out of their wits, they declared the house unfit for human habitation. Mary was a rational woman but she could bear it no longer. The Ricketts moved out.

BAGUIO CITY, PHILIPPINES

Is it possible for an entire city to be haunted? Certainly Baguio City in the Philippines has the reputation of being home to so many wandering souls who cannot rest in peace that they are to be found almost anywhere.

In World War II, the Japanese occupied the city of Baguio. In the heat of war, terrible crimes were perpetrated on the local people. The Laperal White House, a 1920s clapboard house, was used as a garrison by Japanese soldiers. They captured and tortured their enemies here and this barbaric treatment has left its mark. The ghostly apparitions of these poor souls have frequently been seen at the windows of the Laperal House by diners in restaurants across the street. The Teachers' Camp was built in the city in 1908 and used first as a training place for American teachers and then as the Philippine Military Academy in the 1930s. Again, appalling atrocities were committed here during the war. You can rent a cottage on the site today, but people who have, have had horrific haunting experiences, with the victims of violent deaths roaming at large, angry and in search of peace.

The Diplomat Hotel has a different but just as terrible tale to tell. The building was once home to a community of Dominican priests. As the Japanese bombs fell on Baguio, they took refuge here with many others.

The Japanese army burst in and murdered many of its occupants. The house remained abandoned for many years, but people visiting have heard banging doors and screams and have seen the ghosts of headless victims.

Another hotel, the Hyatt, was also the scene of an appalling tragedy. On the 16th July 1990, an earthquake hit the city. Within minutes, the ground beneath the hotel cracked open and the structure came crashing down. Hundreds of people were trapped and many died. This tragic site is closed off today, but people driving past report seeing ghostly figures floating across the zebra crossing behind the locked entrance gates.

†·†·†·†

INSET The faces of tortured prisoners have been seen at the windows of the Laperal White House

RIGHT Today, the Laperal White House is open to the public and contains an art gallery – although many people visit in the hope of encountering the paranormal

CASTLES, FORTRESSES AND PALACES

It isn't surprising that castles, fortresses and palaces should feature prominently in ghostly literature, since these are often places with a very long history. Over countless generations, people have lived, loved, fought, lost and died in these impressive buildings.

One of the most notorious ghosts in British history is Anne Boleyn, the beautiful young wife of Henry VIII, who was beheaded by order of her husband in 1536. Anne grew up at Hever Castle in Kent and her ghost has been seen there sitting beneath a large oak tree in the garden and at a window overlooking the courtyard. The scene of her violent death, however, was the Tower of London, the ultimate fortress. Later we will discuss the legacy she left behind there.

Another of Henry VIII's wives, Catherine Howard, suffered the same fate. She was beheaded in 1542, but before her bloody end she was living with Henry at Hampton Court Palace. When the guards came to arrest her, she ran to the doors of the Chapel Royal where Henry was at prayer and screamed at her husband to show her mercy. None was shown and ever since, people have reported seeing her stricken ghost running along the Gallery.

Corfe Castle in Dorset has an even longer history than Hever and a more grisly past. Once again it's a tale of kings and queens, of treachery and brutality.

In the 12th century, a certain William de Braose, Lord of Bramber, fell out of favour with King John I. As a result, his innocent wife and child were imprisoned at Corfe Castle, where they starved to death. Today, the desperate sounds of a crying child can be heard echoing around the ruins of the castle at all hours.

LEFT
Anne Boleyn was the first, but not the last, of Henry VIII's wives to linger in this world after leaving it so violently

Fortresses, of course, were built to expect violence, so it is no surprise that many have ghostly stories to tell. They have witnessed brutal scenes and miserable deaths through the centuries. For example, Fort William Henry in the state of New York, in the United States, saw a terrible massacre in 1757. British and local troops had been besieged in the Fort by a French army. As the defeated British left the Fort, a group of Native Americans attacked and brutally murdered them, while the French were powerless to stop them. To this day, visitors to the Fort experience mysterious lights and the sounds of soldiers marching, while some of the apparitions actually engage in fighting.

†‡†‡†

ABOVE Corfe Castle is a ruin today, but was home to some horrific tales of cruelty

INTERESTING FACT

THE MOST RECENT SIGHTING OF A GHOST AT CORFE CASTLE WAS IN 1976 WHEN A HEADLESS WOMAN WAS SEEN HOVERING NEAR THE CASTLE GATES.

INTERESTING FACT

THE GHOST OF LADY JANET DOUGLAS, THE LADY OF THE HOUSE IN 1537, HAS BEEN SEEN IN THE CHAPEL AT GLAMIS BY PEOPLE SAYING THEIR PRAYERS.

ABOVE Members of the same family have lived, and died, at Glamis Castle for centuries

INSET There can be few sights more terrifying than that of a silently screaming ghost running through a castle's grounds

GLAMIS CASTLE, SCOTLAND

Glamis Castle in Scotland has all the features of a haunted house. Its looming towers seem to be made for ghosts and ghouls, as though taken from the pages of a fictional ghost story. The truth is, however, that at Glamis the tales become sickeningly real.

Glamis Castle has been the home of the Bowes-Lyon family for more than six centuries. The most famous member of the family was Queen Elizabeth the Queen Mother, wife of King George VI, who was born at Glamis. Long before her time, however, sinister goings-on in the castle left their mark on the place. The ghost of a silently screaming woman with no tongue has been seen in the grounds, pointing to her wounded face. It is said that she stumbled upon the ghastly secret of Glamis, the story that could never be told, a secret that members of the family are sworn to keep. Did this poor servant threaten to reveal all? Did the Earl order the guards to cut out her tongue? Her bloodied ghost suggests just that.

But what is this terrible secret of Glamis? Apparently, it is told to each heir when he comes of age. We can only guess at its horror, but back in 1904, just before the 13th Earl Strathmore died, he apparently confided in a friend that it was so horrifying that, if he knew it, he would get down on his knees and give thanks that it was not his secret.

There is more. The most famous ghost of Glamis is that of Earl Beardie, or Alexander Lindsay, 4th Earl of Crawford. This medieval knight roams the castle in full armour, appearing at children's bedsides and shouting obscenities that can be heard by anyone with the misfortune to be staying there. He was, by all accounts, a nasty character, heavily into gambling and drinking. The story goes that one night he shouted drunkenly for someone to join him in a game of cards. A tall gentleman appeared and together they retired to a room, slammed the door and played all night. A servant looking through the keyhole was blinded by a bright light and in the morning the Earl was dead. The other man, believed to be the Devil himself, had gone, taking the soul of the Earl with him. Some nights, the Earl's ghost is heard shouting behind closed doors, gambling on for all eternity.

CORVIN CASTLE, TRANSYLVANIA

The towers of this enormous castle loom out of the rock it is built on and the whole place is approached by a precarious wooden bridge, perched high above the ground. There is real history behind the scary stories surrounding this place, one of the most haunted castles in the world.

Corvin Castle, also known as Hunyadi Castle, is one of the largest castles in Europe. Built in the 15th century in Hunedoara, Romania, it was the home of the local nobleman, John Hunyadi. What exactly went on here is hard to pin down, but there are many tales of horror and hauntings and certainly anyone visiting has felt the chilly darkness emanating from its walls.

The most famous tale of Corvin involves a 15th-century gruesome, ruthless prince of Wallachia in Romania, known as Vlad the Impaler. His name came from his preferred method for killing his enemies, which was to impale them on sharp stakes. His father, the local ruler, was murdered by a group of noblemen, and Vlad was imprisoned in the castle's dungeon, deep underground. This is a truly eerie, horrible place and the story goes that Vlad gradually went insane down there. Some even claim that he became the bloodthirsty ruler, Count Dracula. Could he be the violent ghost that has been seen wandering the halls and chambers of the castle? This ghoul has certainly been described as vampire-like.

One group of visitors, who dared to stay the night, ran away next morning, utterly terrified, beaten and bruised. They claimed they had been tortured all night by an angry, brutal apparition.

Another tragic tale of the castle concerns the Turkish prisoners who built the well in the central courtyard. They were promised that once they reached water level, they could go free but when, after 15 years' digging, they finally did, the lord of the castle went back on his promise. It is said they cursed the well and all who used it.

INSET This fresco can be found in the Knights' hall in Corvin castle

RIGHT Vlad the Impaler met his end in this picturesque but gruesome place

TOWER OF LONDON, ENGLAND

So many tragic events have happened at the Tower of London that it would be strange if this medieval fortress on the banks of the River Thames was not haunted. For centuries it was the city's strongest and most terrible prison. Countless individuals spent their last weeks and hours in its confines, awaiting their violent and horrible deaths.

The Tower may be a popular tourist destination today, but as the visitors leave and darkness descends, the murky secrets of this place begin to emerge. Some of its long-dead residents, still tortured by the miserable days they spent here, appear to the living once more. Among the Tower's most tragic residents were the young princes, Edward V and his younger brother Richard, Duke of York. On the eve of his coronation in 1483, Edward disappeared and so did his brother. Because Edward was only 13 years old, his uncle, Richard, Duke of Gloucester, was in charge of his welfare. It is widely thought that he had both brothers imprisoned in the Bloody Tower, where they were murdered. He was then crowned King Richard III. These poor children could not find rest, however, and guards have frequently reported seeing two small figures gliding down the stairs of the Bloody Tower.

Another monarch, Anne Boleyn, wife of Henry VIII, was beheaded on Tower Green in 1536, for her infidelity to the king. She was buried under the floor of the Chapel, where her ghost is regularly seen, sometimes with a procession of followers. Many have been terrified to see Anne's headless ghost wandering through the White Tower and the King's House as well, dressed as she was on the day of her execution. One night in 1864, a guard challenged the headless figure, but when he put out his bayonet to stop her it passed right through her.

After Henry's son Edward VI died, Lady Jane Grey ruled as queen for just nine short days. Edward's sister Mary triumphed in her claim to the throne and

LEFT
Prisoners were brought to the Tower of London by boat along the Thames

in 1554, aged only 16, Jane was beheaded on Tower Green. On one anniversary of her death, in 1957, a guard was disturbed by blows on the top of his guardhouse. Going outside, he saw a headless white figure standing on the battlements of the White Tower above him. Scared witless, he called to a fellow guard and they both watched this ghostly apparition in the cold night air.

Perhaps most terrifying of all, the Salt Tower is not somewhere to visit after dark. Indeed, the guards refuse to do just that and dogs will not go near the place at all. Years ago, a guard on patrol was almost strangled by a strong, unseen force there which grabbed him around the neck and held on tight.

ABOVE The ravens at the Tower of London keep watch over its unearthly inhabitants

INTERESTING FACT

MARGARET POLE, COUNTESS OF SALISBURY, WAS SENT TO THE BLOCK IN 1541. SHE ESCAPED AND RAN ROUND TOWER GREEN UNTIL THE EXECUTIONER CAUGHT HER AND CUT OFF HER HEAD.

ABOVE Many generations of people have left their ghostly mark on Edinburgh Castle

INSET Edinburgh is full of tunnels like this one, which can be closed off with a gate

EDINBURGH CASTLE, SCOTLAND

The site of this impressive castle was inhabited long before a chapel dedicated to St Margaret was first built here in the 12th century. Its long history has seen endless tales of suffering and violence and as a result this is a very uncomfortable place indeed to visit after dark.

The castle's location can be eery enough, perched on top of Castle Rock and surrounded by steep cliffs. But deep down below the ground, its dungeons have held hundreds of prisoners in absolute misery and the legacy of their terror remains. Visitors report chillingly cold spots down there, mysterious lights and shadows, and objects shifting around all by themselves. One prisoner tried to escape by hiding in a pile of horse dung. Unfortunately, the dung was thrown down the steep slopes outside and he met his death. Visitors say his ghostly form tries to push them off the battlements and there is an overwhelming whiff of dung in the air.

More creepy still is the ghost of the piper. A series of tunnels runs beneath the castle and across the city. When they were discovered, a piper was sent to explore them, so that the sound of his pipes as he moved forwards would let the people above know where he was. Suddenly, the sound of his pipes stopped. A rescue party sent to look for him found no trace.

He had vanished into thin air and was never seen again. The ghostly sound of his piping is often heard from inside the castle and from the streets above the tunnels.

A second musician haunts this imposing place. A drummer boy is said to appear whenever the castle is in danger. No one knows the story of this headless boy, whose drums were heard in 1650 during the English Civil War, when Cromwell was about to attack.

All the best-haunted castles have an impressive lady ghost, but you would not want to meet Lady Janet Douglas at Edinburgh who also haunts this castle as well as Glamis. Back in 1537, she was accused of witchcraft and conspiracy to murder King James V. Her gruesome fate was to be burned at the stake in the castle on Castle Hill. To add to the horror, her young son was forced to watch from the battlements. Her desperate spirit still wanders through the castle.

ABOVE Visitors to Dover Castle have reported troubling sights and sounds from soldiers who died long ago

DOVER CASTLE, ENGLAND

Dover Castle stands, proud and magnificent, on the south coast of England, looking out across the Channel towards France. In its 800-year history, it has stood as a great bastion, a vital defensive fortress against an array of enemies. No wonder, then, that it is home to so many appearances of the paranormal.

Dover Castle played an important role in World War II, as a labyrinth of underground tunnels that were used for planning the evacuation of thousands of Allied soldiers from Dunkirk and as a command centre for the army, navy and air force. The ghosts of servicemen have often been seen down here in recent decades, some of them walking through solid doors. The air is filled with sounds of banging doors, as if the urgent and tragic business of war was still being conducted.

Other apparitions at Dover have a far longer history. An impressive figure of a 17th-century Cavalier has been seen in several locations around the keep, even in broad daylight. He wears a wide-brimmed black hat, a long purple cloak and his flowing locks and twirling moustache match perfectly the dress of Royalists from this time. Why is he here? He does not shy away from confronting witnesses, but he never seems to threaten them, he just passes by and vanishes.

Upstairs in the kings' bedroom, the lower half of a man floats through the walls. Who knows why this poor soul has only half a body? Perhaps the most poignant and tragic story at Dover Castle is of the drummer boy. This time, there is a story to explain the appearance of this troubled soul. A young drummer called Sean Flynn was sent on an errand into Dover with a large sum of money. He was followed by two soldiers, who grabbed his purse and sliced off his head with a sword. Visitors and staff have heard the sound of slow, mournful drumming in the castle at night and some have even seen the decapitated figure of a boy wandering along the battlements.

INSET Visitors have reported feeling ghostly presences near windows and stairways in Dover Castle

RIGHT Winding stairs inside Dover castle are the perfect haunting ground for ghostly apparitions

AKERSHUS FORTRESS, NORWAY

Norway's capital city, Oslo, is home to the country's most impressive medieval building. Since the 13th century, Akershus Fortress has served as a castle, a prison and even a base for the Nazis during their occupation of Norway during World War II.

Today, the Akershus fortress is used for state occasions, but this eerie place is the most haunted place in Norway and home to some peculiar ghouls.

It is not just tortured human beings who cannot find peace after their deaths. At Akershus, the ghost of a dog has been seen many times. This demon dog is called Malcanisen and is said to guard the main gates to the castle. No one knows why he insists on performing his duties even after death – but the story goes that he was buried alive many centuries ago and that as a result he

carries a deadly curse. Anyone unfortunate enough to catch a glimpse of Malcanisen will suffer a horrible death, and soon.

The other spectre at Akershus Fortress takes human form. She is a lady called Mantelgeisten and she has often been seen emerging in the darkness as if from nowhere, in an area of the fortress called Magaretasalen. This unquiet spirit wears a long, flowing robe and she appears to be making her way back to her chamber. When she turns her head, however, any terrified viewer is greeted by an even more haunting sight – her face is

LEFT
Akershus Fortress looks
forbidding, even on a
fine summer's day

completely blank, with no facial features whatsoever.

This grisly place served as a prison in the 18th and 19th centuries, and in the 20th century the Nazis used it as a place of interrogation, torture and execution, so it is hardly surprising that visitors to Akershus have sensed sinister, unseen forces at work here. They have heard whisperings in corridors, and forces pushing them in the back, as well as the sounds of screams and rattling chains. The centuries of suffering have left a legacy of restless souls that continue to haunt their place of death.

†‡‡†

ABOVE Dark and scary statues, part of a recent art installation, only add to the spooky atmosphere inside the fortress

INTERESTING FACT

IT IS BELIEVED THAT A DOG WAS BURIED ALIVE AT THE ENTRANCE TO AKERSHUS AND ITS GHOST STILL SCARES AWAY INTRUDERS.

INTERESTING FACT

BHANGARH FORT IS SO TERRIFYING THAT THE ARCHAEOLOGICAL SURVEY OF INDIA HAS FORBIDDEN ANYONE TO VENTURE ONTO THE SITE AFTER DARK.

ABOVE Bhangarh Fort is in ruins today, but still attracts visitors who can feel its aura of tragedy

INSET Long, abandoned corridors lie inside the remnants of the Fort

BHANGARH FORT, INDIA

India is a stunningly beautiful country, but its history certainly holds some spooky secrets as well. One of the scariest has to be Bhangarh Fort, in the deserted town of Bhangarh in Rajasthan. This ruin of a place is believed to be the most haunted place in the whole of India.

What makes this place so troubled? There are two main stories to explain the chilling sense of despair and misery reported by visitors. The first concerns the original construction of the fort itself. In 1573, King Madho Singh asked permission to build at Bhangarh from a local ascetic guru called Balu Nath, who would meditate daily at the location. Balu gave the king permission, but on one condition: the shadow of the fort must never fall on his meditation retreat. The guru warned that, if this were to happen, the city would turn to ruins. The king built the fort, but, unwisely, one part of the building did cast a shadow over Balu's place of meditation. Sure enough, the curse came into force and the whole fort crumbled into ruins. Any building work that followed met a similar fate.

The second story is of a beautiful princess and a sorcerer's curse. Princess Ratnavati of Bhangarh was famed for her beauty and Singhia the sorcerer fell in love with her.

He knew he had little chance of winning her hand in marriage, so he hatched a plan to capture her heart. He would cast a spell over the cosmetic oil the princess used on her face, so that when she touched it, she would be overcome with love. It all went wrong, however, as the princess saw him casting the spell and threw the bowl of oil onto the ground. The bowl struck a boulder, which forced it to move. It rolled over the sorcerer and crushed him. As he lay dying, Singhia cursed the entire city of Bhangarh to eternal death.

Visitors to Bhangarh have narrowly avoided death from falling buildings and a chilling sense of hollowness descends on the place after dark. They have felt the eyes of the dead following them and have hurried to escape with the utmost speed.

VERSAILLES, FRANCE

The Palace of Versailles, built by King Louis XIV, is one of the wonders of France, if not of all Europe. Its beauty, however, cannot hide the dark side of the palace's history.

King Louis XIV of France spent a lot of time at Versailles with his wife, Queen Marie Antoinette. As a gift to her he built a separate house in the grounds, called the Petit Trianon. This was her private retreat. It was here that on the 10th August 1792, at the height of the French Revolution, an angry mob stormed in and captured the king and queen. Both were imprisoned and in 1793 they were executed. Just over 100 years later, on the 10th August 1901, two women from Oxford University were visiting Versailles on holiday. What they saw became one of the most extraordinary ghost stories of the 20th century.

Walking through the park in search of the Petit Trianon, the two women, Anne Moberly and Eleanor Jourdain, saw two men with long green coats and three-cornered hats, who seemed to be gardeners. An old plough lay by the side of the road. At a gazebo, Miss Moberly saw a man with a scarred face, who directed them across a bridge. On arriving at the Petit Trianon, Miss Moberly saw a footman and a seated woman in fine but old fashioned clothes, sketching. Throughout their walk, both women had a deep sense of unease, of foreboding and gloom.

It was only when, back in Oxford, Miss Moberly mentioned the people she had seen that the pair realised they had been visible only to her – Miss Jourdain saw nobody. When they discovered that the day of their visit was exactly 109 years after the attack by the mob, they were seriously afraid, but also curious. Investigating further, they learned that in 1901 there was neither gazebo, nor bridge, nor footman, nor green-coated gardeners at Versailles – and the striking woman was dressed exactly as Marie Antoinette had been in a painted portrait. All those features had, however, been present in 1792. Was this a time-slip experience? Could that have explained their deep sense of gloom, that death was approaching for the French queen?

INSET The Petit Trianon was a private retreat for Queen Marie Antoinette (right), but it could not protect her from the angry mob and a gruesome death

OUTDOOR PLACES AROUND THE WORLD

You might think that the world's open spaces would be free of troubled spirits, that the healthy, vitalising power of nature would cleanse away any vestiges of the paranormal, but you would be wrong. Wherever men and women have set foot, it seems they have left their ghostly mark.

The English Home Counties feel like gentle, benign places and not the most obvious locations for spying ghosts. In Buckinghamshire, however, in the Hughenden Valley near High Wycombe, several people have had a frightening encounter with an inexplicable presence. The forest here is said to be haunted by a green man. Folklore about the Green Man, a pagan fertility spirit, goes back centuries and in medieval times he was often depicted as a head without a body. In 1986, a man driving home encountered a figure dressed in green by the side of the road; a figure that disappeared as suddenly as it had emerged. Reading of this in the newspaper prompted another local to come forwards. He, too, had seen a green figure in the exact same spot, waving its arms as he drove towards it, as if in warning of danger ahead. As he approached, it vanished.

A long way from the rolling hills of England, out in the desert of Namibia, is Kolmanskop. This was once a centre for mining diamonds, but today the ruins of the settlement are being reclaimed not only by the sand, but by the spirits of its former residents. The vast landscape dwarfs the skeletons of the buildings, and the wind blows sand through them in drifts. This is a ghost town in more sense than one, however, as its former residents have been seen flitting through the open doorways and desolate spaces of a place that is slowly, slowly, returning to nature.

Over in the United States, the Olympic National Park in Washington also has a multitude of ghosts and paranormal activities to its credit. The 13 km (8 mile) Spruce Railroad Trail is particularly

LEFT
The Green Man is a prominent figure in English folklore

chilling, according to hikers who have returned from it deeply shaken.

In 1937, a woman called Hallie Illingworth was murdered here by her brutal husband. Her body remained undiscovered for several years, so perhaps it is not surprising she could not rest in peace. Finally, in 1940, a mummified body bound with ropes floated to the surface of Lake Crescent. It was eventually identified as Hallie and her husband was sent to prison. Ever since then, visitors passing beside the lake have heard a woman screaming and they sometimes see a female figure, dressed in white.

Read on to find out about the desperate souls reaching out to us on the world's highest mountain, at ancient landmarks, in forests and tunnels. What is it they are trying to tell us?

INTERESTING FACT

IN 1912, THE KOLMANSKOP AREA PRODUCED ONE MILLION CARATS OF DIAMONDS BEFORE ITS DEMISE IN THE 1930S.

ABOVE Climbing Mount Everest is the ultimate challenge, but for many, it is the last challenge they will ever take on

INSET These mountaineers are climbing up the Khumbu Icefall on the route up Everest

MOUNT EVEREST, NEPAL

Ever since Tenzing Norgay and Sir Edmund Hillary first reached the summit of Mount Everest, in 1953, there have been strange stories of the ghostly and the supernatural from the men and women who have risked everything to achieve their goal.

On the highest reaches of Mount Everest, death is a constant possibility. Hundreds of climbers have died here and because of the challenging conditions it is not usually possible to retrieve their bodies. There they lie, frozen in time. In 2009, a Tibetan Sherpa called Pemba Dorje was nearing the summit when a series of ghostly black shapes reached out to him, as if begging for food. As he moved past them, they vanished. A few years earlier, in 1996, a climber called Jon Krakauer was descending Everest after reaching the summit. He was not surprised to see his fellow climber Andy Harris beside him – until he later learned that Harris had been killed, along with eight other climbers, in a terrible storm nearer the summit.

Two British climbers told the tale of a famous ghost from the past that sustained them in their terrifying ordeal on the mountain. In 1975, Dougal Haston and Doug Scott became the first British men to reach the summit. Before their triumph, however, they spent an anxious night in a snow-hole camp below it and it was here that they both reported feeling some kind of benign presence with them. Next day, as they strived for the summit, this presence remained with them, encouraging them towards their success. Was this the spirit of Andrew Irvine, the 22-year-old British climber who in 1924 made an attempt on the mountain with George Mallory? No one knows if Mallory and Irvine ever reached the summit, but if they did it was their final act, as they disappeared without trace. Mallory's broken body was finally discovered in 1999, but Irvine has never been found and remains where he fell to his death. Was he seeking to help his fellow Englishmen in their quest for the summit, to complete the task he was so tragically denied?

STONEHENGE, ENGLAND

If hauntings and paranormal events are most likely to take place in locations with a long history, then Stonehenge must surely be one of the most haunted places on Earth.

This circle of massive stones set on the open plains of Wiltshire dates back between four and five thousand years. Its whole existence is suffused with mystery. We do not know for certain why it was erected. Was it to be a burial ground or a place of worship? Was it a place of healing or of ritual to mark the passing of the seasons or to connect with spirits from another world? The culture that created this massive structure left no written records and so the stones must speak for themselves.

People who are lucky enough to visit Stonehenge after the crowds of tourists have departed report a definite sense of the unworldly here. Evidence of cremation burials has been found on the site, proving that many funerary rites were performed here many thousands of years ago, so the spirits of these ancient souls may well still linger.

In the summer of 2017, a group of researchers were investigating the appearance of crop circles on land nearby. As they filmed a huge field, a mysterious figure appeared, standing in the middle of the tall wheat. There it stood for 20 minutes without moving, but when they turned the camera away from it towards the edge of the field, the figure disappeared. In such a large field, a person could not have run away out of sight in the time it took them to bring the camera back to the same spot.

A much more scary story dates from August 1971, when the stones of Stonehenge were still open to all. A group of people decided to pitch their tents for the night right among the stones. In the middle of the night a thunderstorm blew in and lightning struck the stones. A farmer and a policeman in the area reported seeing an eerie blue light around the stone circle, one so bright they had to look away. They heard wild screaming from the campers and ran to find out what was happening. When they arrived, they were shocked to the core – the campers had completely vanished, tents and all. No trace of them was ever found.

RIGHT In earlier times, people could roam among the stones, but for some this was an unworldly experience

Gravestones:

BESSIE
THE DEAR WIFE OF
ALEX* G. HOLT.
DIED 28TH NOV* 1921.
...CHRIST WHICH IS FAR BETTER
ALSO OF
...XANDER GOODE HOLT.
...11TH FEBRUARY 1938.
...AGED 91 YEARS
...LIVE UNTO GOD.

ANNIE.
THE DEARLY LOVED WIFE OF
THOMAS RICHARD HOLT.
WHO DIED ON TUESDAY EVENING
8TH MARCH 1898
BUT ALIVE UNTO GOD THROUGH JESUS CHRIST
ALSO OF
THOMAS RICHARD HOLT.
WHO DIED 10TH MARCH 1913.
ALL HEARTS AND TRUE STAND EVER WITH THE LORD.
W. ROLAND SUTTON.
MUCH LOVED BY HIS WIFE MARJORIE
AND HIS DAUGHTER PAMELA
1905 - 6TH JUNE 1994.
ALSO OF THEIR GRANDSON RALPHIE,
INFANT SON OF RALPH AND JOSEPHINE HOLT,
WHO DIED 14TH DECEMBER 1904.
AGED 8 MONTHS.
WITHOUT FAULT BEFORE THE THRONE OF GOD.
THOMAS JAMES HOLT, ELDEST SON
DIED 12TH JAN. 1934.
RALPH JESSE FLUKER HOLT, YOUNGEST
DIED 13TH JAN. 1932.
BOTH INTERRED AT SCARBOROUGH.
JOHN HENRY SUTTON, SON-IN-LAW
DIED 13TH NOV. 1933.
MABEL CLAIRE SUTTON.

INTERESTING FACT

KARL MARX IS ONE OF THE MOST FAMOUS RESIDENTS OF THE CEMETERY. BUT ONLY A MISERLY 11 PEOPLE WERE PRESENT AT HIS BURIAL.

ABOVE The dilapidated and overgrown state of Highgate Cemetery only adds to its creepy atmosphere, yet hundreds of visitors still come to see the grave of Karl Marx (inset)

HIGHGATE CEMETERY, LONDON

Well what do you expect in a cemetery? The last resting places of the dead might be expected to hold a few unquiet spirits, but at Highgate Cemetery in north London there have been dozens of sightings of a far more sinister apparition.

In Victorian times, Highgate Cemetery was the smartest place to be buried if you were a Londoner of note. Thousands of the capital's most famous residents were interred here, such as the author George Eliot, poet Christina Rossetti and philosopher Karl Marx. In the 20th century, it fell into disrepair, however, and the beautiful monuments became overgrown and dilapidated. That was when the sinister stories began.

In the 1960s, the first accounts emerged of a tall, dark figure hanging around in and near the cemetery. This was no 'ordinary' ghost. His feet never touched the ground, his eyes glowed red and his ashen face was contorted into a terrifying visage – that of a vampire. This terrifying ghoul was no passive spectre, either. He has wreaked havoc in Highgate for decades, threatening the local population, knocking people to the ground, freezing them in their tracks – and disappearing through solid walls.

More recently he has ventured beyond the cemetery, to the Flask public house and a block of flats known as Hillcrest. Here, too, there are reports of the temperature suddenly dropping, clocks stopping for no reason and objects appearing to crash off shelves to the floor.

The spirit of an old lady also haunts the land of Highgate Cemetery. She runs wildly through the cemetery, between the mossy, overgrown monuments and gravestones, apparently searching for her children who, it is said, she brutally murdered. Another figure joins her sometimes, but this is a quiet presence, a shrouded figure who stands staring up into the sky. Approach her and she vanishes – but you will soon see her a little way off, gazing again at the heavens as if searching for an answer to an age-old question.

AOKIGAHARA FOREST, JAPAN

This densely wooded forest at the base of beautiful Mount Fuji in Japan is a sad, sad place. It is where many Japanese people have been left to die or, more recently, have chosen to take their own lives. No wonder, then, that Aokigahara Forest, which is also known as the Sea of Trees, is said to be populated with lost souls.

In 1960, a novel by Japanese author Seicho Matsumoto was published. His story tells of a pair of young lovers who commit suicide in the forest and it became a bestseller. Ever since then, dozens of people have taken this tragic course there every year, although many are believed to have died in the forest previously. Signs around the forest remind people that their life is a precious gift and to consider their families. Sometimes, however, this is not enough.

People visiting the forest to walk and enjoy the beautiful trees report that it feels overwhelmingly sad. It is also very easy to get lost and to spend time there after dark is not a pleasant experience. Many of the troubled spirits of the recently deceased seem to be lingering here. Officials caution against deviating from the main paths, not least because some strange magnetic activity in the forest seems to make it almost impossible to find your way out, once you are lost.

LEFT
Finding your way through the forest's dense trees and undergrowth is a challenge even in daylight

The ghostly history of Aokigahara Forest reaches further back even than the decades since the 1960s. In ancient times, this was a place where the Japanese would abandon people to die. In times of famine or other hopeless trouble, families would leave their children or elderly relatives here, because there was no food for them and these wretched individuals would suffer a horrible, slow death by starvation. The forest is said to be haunted by these poor souls. Perhaps in their misery they have also had a part to play in attracting desperate living souls to the forest, to join them in eternity.

ABOVE A shot of Aokigahara Forest in twilight, perfectly capturing the gloomy nature of the forest where so many go to end their lives

INTERESTING FACT

ABOUT 70 CORPSES ARE REMOVED FROM AOKIGAHARA FOREST EACH YEAR AND MANY MORE ARE NEVER FOUND.

SCREAMING TUNNEL, NIAGARA, CANADA

Niagara Falls is one of the great wonders of the world, but it is also home to an awesome secret. Most visitors to this incredible attraction never get to know about this chilling story.

The Grand Trunk Railway line used to run along the north-west corner of Niagara Falls. Beneath it sits a narrow tunnel, built in the early 1800s, just 5 m (16 ft) high and 38 m (125 ft) long. It was not a railway tunnel; it carried surplus water down to the valley below and the local people used it to transport goods and animals safely under the busy railway. This apparently harmless structure is, however, known as the Screaming Tunnel and it has a terrible past.

About 100 years ago, a local girl died in this confined space. There are several versions of her tragic story.

One says she lived on a nearby farm and one night escaped from one of the barns when it accidentally caught fire. Her clothes were ablaze and, desperate and in pain, she ran to the tunnel thinking that the water in it would help to put the fire out. It was too late, however, and she died screaming as the fire consumed her. In another version, she was set on fire by her father. He was consumed by fury when his wife refused him custody of their children after their divorce and in a fit of madness turned that fury on his innocent daughter.

Whatever the truth of this, her piercing screams and her terrible death remained the same.

Ever since, people visiting the tunnel after dark have been chilled by sounds of a young girl's screams. It is said that if you stand in the middle of the tunnel at night, and light a match, the flame terrifies the spirit of this poor girl and her screams ring through the tunnel for all to hear.

†+‡+†

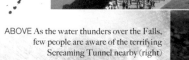

ABOVE As the water thunders over the Falls, few people are aware of the terrifying Screaming Tunnel nearby (right)

EPPING FOREST, UK

A densely wooded forest is not a place to linger at night. The deep shadows hold unknown terrors and the whispering trees speak of spirits at loose among their branches. If that woodland is Epping Forest, in Essex, there are even more reasons to stay well away.

Back in the 18th century, Epping Forest was a notoriously dangerous place. This was the hangout of highwaymen and thieves, murderers and criminals of all kinds. The most infamous highwayman of the time was Dick Turpin and Epping was his patch. As travellers passed through the wood on horseback or in a carriage, he would leap out at them from the cover of the trees and demand their valuables at gunpoint. Turpin did not stop at robbery, however. He murdered at least one man in Epping Forest and for his crimes he was eventually hanged, in York in 1739. His imposing ghost, dressed in a long cloak and wide-brimmed hat, has been seen in the forest many times, leading walkers off the path and into the depths of the undergrowth, until they are well and truly lost.

Turpin's victims cannot rest in peace either. Back in the 1920s, one terrified observer told the tale of his journey through the forest with a friend. Cycling along a track, they clearly heard the sound of horses and a carriage approaching them from behind. As the creaking of the carriage and the clatter of hooves grew louder and louder, the two men stopped to let them pass. As they turned around to look, the sounds continued – but there was nothing there.

LEFT
Many of the trees in Epping Forest are hundreds of years old

There was one particular area of the forest that Turpin made his base and that was Loughton Camp. This creepy place has an even longer history and an even more violent one. This is the place where Queen Boudica, queen of the Iceni tribe of Britons, made the base for her army during the fight with the Romans in AD 60. Fearless Boudica marched her soldiers into battle against the occupying Romans, but they were defeated and hacked down. Many people think that the spirits of her fearful soldiers as they contemplated defeat on the eve of battle linger in this gloomy place.

ABOVE The infamous highwayman Dick Turpin shoots a victim in Epping Forest, from his hideaway at Loughton Camp

INTERESTING FACT

A POND WITHIN THE FOREST DRAWS PEOPLE TO THEIR DEATHS. IT IS THE SITE OF A TRAGIC MURDER-SUICIDE OF TWO YOUNG LOVERS 300 YEARS AGO.

INTERESTING FACT

VOYAGERS BELIEVED
THE GREAT EASTERN
WAS CURSED. ON ITS
ARRIVAL IN NEW YORK
CITY, ITS PADDLE
WHEEL SHEARED 1.5 M
(5 FT) OFF THE DOCK.

ABOVE A stormy sea is a terrifying place, but even more so when the people whose lives it claims cannot rest in peace

INSET The *Great Eastern* is shown here in all its splendour in this engraved illustration

ALL AT SEA

Ever since men first set out to sea, sailing the seas has been dangerous. No wonder, then, that there are tales of tragedy on the ocean waves that have left behind a ghostly legacy. Whole ships have vanished into thin air. Others appear mysteriously as if from nowhere – after they have sunk.

In 1893, the Royal Navy's leading battleship was HMS *Victoria*, a fine vessel with a large crew. Its commander was no less a figure than Admiral Sir George Tryon, who had a reputation as a daring and highly capable handler of his ships. In June that year, while on manoeuvres near Tripoli in Lebanon, the *Victoria* collided with another British ship, HMS *Camperdown*. Within minutes, the stricken ship filled up with water and sank, taking hundreds of crew members with her. Tryon remained on board to the end and was heard by several survivors to say 'It was entirely my fault, all my fault.' Back in London, Tryon's wife was having a large party at the time of this tragedy. Several of her guests were amazed to see their hostess's husband, Admiral Sir George Tryon, descending the staircase of the couple's home. Only later did they learn that this had been at the exact moment that the *Victoria* went down, taking the Admiral to the bottom of the sea.

The *Great Eastern* was another Victorian vessel with a sad story. Built in 1857, it was the largest ship ever made and from the beginning it seemed destined for trouble.

At its launch it became jammed and on its maiden voyage a ventilator exploded, killing several of the crew. It suffered numerous accidents and on many of its voyages crew members reported hearing a strange hammering noise from far below decks. This could even be heard above the noises of a storm and would wake sailors from their sleep. When the ship was eventually retired and sold for scrap metal, a possible source of this phantom hammering was discovered: between the two layers of its double hull was a skeleton of a man. This could only be the master shipwright, who had mysteriously disappeared during the ship's construction many years earlier.

Where else have the waves claimed lives, only for them to live on, in limbo, to make contact with the living? Ghostly sightings abound on the Island of Dolls in Mexico, on trans-Atlantic liners and in St Augustine's Lighthouse in Florida. Read on to discover their harrowing tales.

ISLAND OF THE DOLLS, MEXICO

Just south of Mexico City lies an island; a sad and creepy place, which today is visited by hundreds of travellers, but which was never intended to be a tourist destination. This is the Island of the Dolls.

Back in the 1950s, a young man named Julian Santana Barrera left his wife and young family and moved to this small island to be a recluse. He was unaware of the tragedy that had taken place there, but he soon came to know of it all too well. Stories vary, but one describes how, in the 1920s, three young girls had been playing at the water's edge. One of them fell in and drowned. Locals claimed that ever since that day, the spirit of this young girl had remained on the island, unable to find peace. They refused to set foot there after dark.

Julian, however, soon found that the young spirit began talking to him. She told him what had happened and appeared to be trapped in the place of her death. One day, Julian found an old doll floating in the water. He knew it must have belonged to the lost girl and hung it up to appease her spirit. The haunting intensified however, becoming ever more relentless, so Julian bought more dolls, selling the food he managed to grow in an attempt to ease this troubled spirit's way to peace.

After many years, the island was covered with dolls, hanging from every tree. Julian felt that the spirit of this tragic figure possessed the dolls themselves. He told his nephew that she was becoming harder to appease and he feared that she wanted him to join her on the other side. A short time later, Julian was found dead, floating face down in the water, in exactly the same place where the girl had died so many years before.

Today, the island is a terrifying place. The eyes of hundreds of dismembered dolls seem to follow you around and some visitors have heard them whispering, especially after dark. There are reports that Julian's ghost wanders the island, too, still unable to leave behind the girl he tried so hard to save.

✝✝✝✝✝

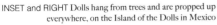

INSET and RIGHT Dolls hang from trees and are propped up everywhere, on the Island of the Dolls in Mexico

RMS QUEEN MARY, USA

In her time, the RMS *Queen Mary* was one of the most luxurious liners in the world. This magnificent ship, launched in 1936, transported world leaders, Hollywood stars and royalty across the ocean between the US and England. However, some on board refuse to leave, even after death.

A young crewman called John Henry met his end in a horrifying ordeal on board the *Queen Mary*. He worked in engine room 13, where one day a fire broke out. As he tried to flee, he was crushed to death. Ever since, there have been reports of knocks and bright lights in engine room 13, even screams and smoke emanating from it and sometimes the door to it is so hot to touch that it burns your fingers.

In 1966, a 17-year-old fireman called John Pedder was working on board. He was tragically crushed to death by a watertight door during a routine drill. Again, knocking has been heard here and a darkly dressed figure has been seen walking along before disappearing through the door.

A luxury swimming pool up on deck sounds like an idyllic place to linger, but this creepy place is not for the faint-hearted. The pool has been empty for many years – so how can wet footprints appear beside it, heading for the changing rooms? Could this be the spirit of a woman who was once murdered in these very changing rooms?

LEFT
The RMS *Queen Mary* offered its passengers the last word in luxury, but was also the scene of awful tragedies

She is not alone. A little girl drowned in the pool in the ship's sailing days and people have seen her, carrying her teddy bear, at the poolside. Her voice joins those of other invisible swimmers and the sounds of splashing water.

It seems luxury could not preserve travellers from tragedy. In the first-class staterooms, a beautiful woman in a long white gown dances alone in a shadowy corner, while a man in a 1930s style suit appears, making the lights turn on and off of their own accord. The telephone rings in the early morning, but there is nobody on the other end.

The *Queen Mary* is now permanently moored as a tourist attraction in Long Beach, California, where its ghosts no doubt still roam.

ABOVE The First Class accommodation was as lavish as any luxury hotel, but some passengers were never able to check out

INTERESTING FACT

DURING WORLD WAR II, THE *QUEEN MARY* COLLIDED WITH *HMS CURACAO*, SLICING THAT SHIP IN TWO. HUNDREDS OF SAILORS DROWNED.

ABOVE At St Augustine's Lighthouse in Florida, the Pity girls seem
reluctant to leave the place where they met their tragic deaths

INSET The top of the lighthouse, with its spectacular view, is the
favourite haunt of its previous occupants

ST AUGUSTINE'S LIGHTHOUSE

In Florida, in the southern states of the US, St Augustine's Lighthouse began guiding ships at sea away from treacherous rocks back in 1874. Today, the lighthouse and the keeper's house attract visitors, rather than ships, and all because of their ghostly history.

One of the first keepers of the lighthouse was Peter Rasmussen, a highly skilled man who performed his duties with great care. He loved to smoke cigars – and in the years since his death both staff and visitors have smelled the aroma of cigar smoke wafting around the lighthouse. Another keeper was Joseph Andreu.

He was painting the outside of the tower one day when the scaffolding he was standing on collapsed and he fell to his death. It seems poor Joseph was reluctant to leave his post, however, as he is often seen looking out from the top of the lighthouse tower.

The most harrowing tale of this seaside place, however, concerns Hezekiah Pity and his two young daughters, Eliza and Mary. Hezekiah was supervising building work at the lighthouse, but his children were bored. They climbed inside a cart that was being used to carry materials back and forth to the site. When the cart broke loose from its tracks, it plunged headlong into the bay. Workers rushed to save the children, but it was too late and they drowned in the sea. The girls still love this place, however, and are regularly seen and heard laughing at the top of the tower. Eliza appears all around the site, still wearing the beautiful blue velvet dress in which she died.

Other mysterious events have attracted attention – and anxiety – at the lighthouse. The staff lock the door carefully every night, yet frequently they find it open in the morning. Furniture moves to new positions unbidden and music boxes begin to play. The temperature has been known to plummet in certain areas and figures appear, only to vanish in the blink of an eye. The ships at sea may be safe, but anyone visiting this profoundly haunted place must feel anything but.

REAL-LIFE GHOST STORIES

In 2002, two motorists on the A3 in Surrey called the police to report a crash. They had both seen a maroon car veering off the road ahead of them. When the police arrived at the scene, however, they could find no signs of a crash – until they looked a little further...

Sure enough, as they looked down into a ditch, there was a maroon Vauxhall Astra, nose down. But it was covered with undergrowth and had clearly been there for several months. To their horror, inside they found the decomposed body of the driver.

Had this poor individual come back to show others the way to his final resting place, so he could finally be laid to rest?

Stories such as this one capture the imagination and continue people's interest in the supernatural and paranormal, especially when facts and weird coincidences play such a lead role. Sometimes it can be difficult to separate the truth from what may be the overactive imagination of a witness.

It is hard to deny, though, that something often leads us to question the existence and nature of an afterlife.

Read on for more real-life ghost stories and make up your own mind about them. Does Lincoln still reside in The White House more than 150 years after his infamous assassination? Is Disneyland inhabited by spirits who linger on? Are some of London's West End theatres haunted? Let's find out.

††‡†

INSET and RIGHT It is easy to forget that the places we love to visit once offered comfort - or not - to others. When the unexplained appears before us, it can be truly terrifying

POLTERGEISTS

A poltergeist is a very distinctive kind of ghost. Poltergeists can be violent. They seem determined to attract our attention and cause chaos. Is this a reflection of a violent life or death? Certainly, living with a poltergeist can be hellish and utterly terrifying.

Poltergeists make noises; they bang and thud walls and they slam doors. They also move things around, shifting furniture and throwing small objects across the room. The effects of these unquiet spirits are plain to see.

Another feature of poltergeists is that they often appear in very ordinary houses, not necessarily historic palaces and castles. One of the most terrifying cases of poltergeist haunting was on an ordinary street in Yorkshire. Number 30 East Drive in Pontefract stood close to the site of the old town gallows. In the 1960s, it was the home of the Pritchard family. One afternoon, puddles of water began appearing on the kitchen floor.

The water board came to investigate, but they could find no cause and the water kept on appearing. Later that evening, young Philip Pritchard was being looked after by his grandmother, who both watched in horror as sugar and tea were strewn around the kitchen – by nobody visible. The lights came on in the hall and a potted plant made its own way up the stairs. Back in the kitchen, the crockery in the cupboard began to clatter uncontrollably. For some strange reason, the pair of them decided to go to bed, only to find the chest of drawers swaying in the corner of the bedroom. That was the final straw and they left to stay with neighbours.

LEFT
When everyday objects appear to be possessed, it's probably time to go

When they returned, the activity stopped abruptly. All was quiet for two years but it began again, this time Diane Pritchard, the daughter, was the target. On one occasion she was thrown from her bed in the middle of the night, another time she was dragged up the stairs by her throat. Who knows why the family did not flee. A concerned family friend doused holy water through the house – whereupon the spirit painted upside down crucifixes on the walls and doors. Only when this tortured ghost finally appeared did these horrendous manifestations stop. Mr and Mrs Pritchard finally saw the figure of a hooded monk in their bedroom. In the 16th century, a monk was hanged at the nearby gallows for the murder of a local girl. This seemed to be the source of their malevolent poltergeist.

✝✝✝✝

ABOVE The monk in the Pritchard's house had been present at the site for 500 years

INTERESTING FACT

WE CAN SEE THE EFFECTS THAT POLTERGEISTS HAVE ON A PLACE, BUT UNLIKE OTHER GHOSTS, WE ALMOST NEVER SEE THEIR ACTUAL FORM.

ABOVE Rosenheim is a pretty town, but Annemarie Schaberl (inset) brought
terrifying paranormal activity to her office there in the late 1960s

THE ROSENHEIM POLTERGEIST

Poltergeists do not confine their activity to houses. One of the most famous cases of poltergeist activity happened in an office building. Read on to see if you would work in the world's spookiest office.

The scene of this horror was an office in Rosenheim, Bavaria, in Germany. This poltergeist seemed to enjoy using electricity and telephones to wreak havoc. In 1967, the office began to experience spontaneous explosions of light bulbs and electrical fuses. Then the telephones would all start to ring at once, but when they were answered there was never anybody on the other end. Engineers installed a separate power unit to the office in case a power surge was causing the electrical problems, but the happenings continued. Telephone bills for the office showed that hundreds of calls were being made – mostly to the speaking clock. What's more, far more calls were being made in a short time than was physically possible using the old dial telephones. What was going on?

When monitoring equipment was brought into the office, it emerged that this disturbing activity only occurred when one particular employee was at work. Annemarie Schaberl was 19 years old and as she arrived and walked down the corridor, lights would switch on and off above her head. Filing cabinet drawers would open unbidden and pictures fell of the wall. This bizarre activity was witnessed by many people and recorded by a string of experts, including electrical engineers, police officers and physicists, not to mention investigators of the paranormal.

Not surprisingly, Annemarie decided to leave her job. No doubt her colleagues were glad to see her go, as the poltergeist disturbances immediately stopped. Further investigation showed that Annemarie was a troubled teenager and that similar activity had been happening at her previous jobs. She finally found happiness and got married in 1969 – and all paranormal activity around her ceased. Some think she had been generating such psychic energy that she had activated the poltergeist activity. When she matured and settled down, that energy ebbed away and peace descended once more.

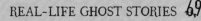

LINCOLN IN THE WHITE HOUSE

The White House in Washington, DC, is the official home of the President of the United States. Over the centuries, presidents have come and gone – except that some of them clearly have not gone that far.

Ghostly sightings of the building's previous residents have been surprisingly frequent, to the point where some visitors have asked to be moved and many recent presidents have described feeling the presence of their predecessors.

The first president to occupy the White House was John Adams. He and his wife Abigail moved in, in 1800. The following year, the Adams moved out and Thomas Jefferson moved in. Abigail must have had a great fondness for the house, however, as her ghost has been seen carrying laundry to the East Room – and vanishing through the walls.

The most impressive story of White House ghosts, however, has to be that of Abraham Lincoln, the 16th President of the United States. Lincoln was assassinated in 1865, at the end of the American Civil War, a highly troubled time for him and the whole nation. During World War II, another traumatic time, his ghost was repeatedly seen by President Roosevelt wandering through the White House. It was the Lincoln Bedroom, however, that he seemed to prefer. One night during the War, British Prime Minister Winston Churchill was staying at the White House in the

Lincoln Bedroom. He liked to have a long hot bath before bed and on this night he climbed out of the bath and walked, naked, into the bedroom. There he saw the figure of Lincoln, standing by the fireplace. With only a moment's hesitation Churchill spoke, 'Good evening Mr President, you seem to have me at a disadvantage.' The ghostly figure smiled softly at him and disappeared. Had the old leader come back to comfort and support the modern man, in another time of war and strain? Whatever was happening, despite his extraordinarily calm, and witty, response to the apparition, Churchill asked to be moved to another room.

INSET The beautiful interior of the White House is not your typical haunted house

RIGHT Abraham Lincoln has appeared to a number of prominent guests at the White House

LONDON UNDERGROUND

The tube network runs deep below the streets of the capital. Built in the 19th and 20th centuries, it cut through many historic sites, disturbing places and people laid to rest many years before. It is hardly surprising that it harbours some truly scary real-life ghost stories.

In November 1897, William Terris was fatally stabbed on The Strand, near Covent Garden tube station. He had been an actor and often visited the bakery that stood on the site where the station was built soon after he died. One November night in 1955, Jack Hayden, the manager of the station, was locking up when he saw a tall man in an old-fashioned suit walking towards the stairs. He rang up to the ticket office to tell them to expect this last passenger and let him out, but no one ever emerged. Jack and his colleagues searched the station together, but found nobody. A few evenings later, Jack saw the man again. And Jack was not the only one to see him. A young porter got the fright of his life when he approached a tall, well-dressed gentleman in the staff room – who vanished before his eyes. The two men decided to report what they had seen and a sketch was made of their stranger. When they searched through photographs of Victorian figures associated with Covent Garden they both picked out an image of the same man – William Terris.

LEFT
Covent Garden
Underground station
stands on the site of a
terrible murder

In World War II, tube stations were used as air raid shelters for local people as German bombs fell on London. One tragic night, in 1943, as people ran down into Bethnal Green station in East London seeking shelter, a woman and her child tripped on the stairs and fell. The crowd pouring into the station then fell on them and in the terrible pile-up, 173 people were crushed to death, including 62 children. Ever since then, staff working late at night at Bethnal Green station have reported hearing the heartbreaking sounds of children crying, followed by running and screaming.

†‡‡†

ABOVE Stations are packed with passengers by day, but once the gates are locked and night descends, the dark tunnels and long passages are perfect locations for a haunting

INTERESTING FACT

WILLIAM TERRIS ALSO HAUNTS THE ADELPHI THEATRE IN LONDON WHERE HE WAS DUE TO PERFORM ON THE NIGHT OF HIS MURDER.

ABOVE The Haunted Mansion at Disneyland in California seems to have become the residence for genuine lost souls

INSET The Hall of Portraits in the Haunted Mansion is designed to scare, even without the potential for a real-life ghostly apparition

DISNEYLAND GHOSTS

A place of fun and entertainment, which brings happiness to thousands of children and their families every year, is not the kind of place you would expect to be haunted. Yet Disneyland has more ghost stories associated with it than any other tourist attraction in the US.

On the other hand, if you are going to build a Haunted Mansion, what do you expect? Several ghosts are seen regularly here by staff and visitors and not the ones created as part of the attraction. Next to the exit sits a young boy, who weeps uncontrollably. The story goes that this poor child died while still very young. He had loved the Haunted Mansion when he was alive, so his poor mother asked Disneyland if she could scatter his ashes close by. The authorities refused, but one night she sneaked into the ride after it was closed and scattered his remains near the exit. His ghostly presence has remained there ever since.

One night, an employee working in the loading area of the Mansion saw a man in a suit who was holding a cane in his hand. He was sitting in one of the Doom Buggies that goes around the house. When the employee tried to speak to him, there was no reply, and slowly the apparition faded to nothingness. In the 1940s, before Disneyland was built, a pilot crashed his small plane into a lake near the site of the Haunted Mansion. He was killed instantly, but he was known to walk with a cane. Over the years he has been seen quite often, frequenting the place where he met his sad end.

Knowing all that, who would willingly enter the Haunted Mansion for fun? Yet there is more. A sound designer working on the attraction was terrified to hear strange music coming from behind one of the walls. He assumed there must be a radio in there, but for several days the music played without ceasing – then abruptly stopped.

Lastly, a man in a tuxedo seems to have made his spirit home there. An attendant standing at the end of the ride could see riders arriving behind her, in a mirror. She kept seeing the tall figure of a man dressed for an evening out, yet when she turned around there was no-one there. When she felt a chill and a hand on her shoulder, that was it – she walked out and handed in her notice.

HELLFIRE CAVES, ENGLAND

This mysterious complex of caves in Buckinghamshire, England was commissioned by a local aristocrat, Sir Francis Dashwood, in 1752. Caves can be creepy at the best of times, but this place has seen some serious haunting.

There was a natural cave system here already, but Sir Francis wanted to extend them so that they reached further into the darkness for at least half a mile.

Deep underground, a long winding passage leads to a chamber known as the Banqueting Hall, then on to the Inner Temple. This was where Sir Francis wanted to hold meetings with his friends in the Hellfire Club; wild sessions of drinking and debauchery, combined with rituals celebrating the occult. One member of the club was Paul Whitehead, a famous poet of the day.

In a macabre pact, the poet asked Sir Francis that his heart be cut out after his death and placed in an urn in the caves. When his friend died, Sir Francis duly obliged and the urn remained there for many years. Paul Whitehead, however, could not rest at peace without his heart, it seems. His ghost has been seen wandering through the Hellfire Caves, looking for it for all eternity.

He is joined in this murky place by another spirit, called Sukie, sometimes spelt as Suki. Many visitors have seen her in the Banqueting Hall or have heard her piercing screams coming from there. Poor Sukie was a chambermaid in the local inn, the George and Dragon. She longed to marry a man of higher status than herself, so when she received an invitation to meet a wealthy local man at the caves, she eagerly turned up dressed for her wedding day. Of course, it had all been a joke by some local boys and in the fight that ensued Sukie was tragically killed by a blow to the head. Her ghostly apparition, still dressed for her wedding, haunts the creepy tunnels to this day.

RIGHT The long, winding passage that leads to the Banqueting Hall

INSET The tunnels look even creepier after dark

THE STOCKHOLM GHOST TRAIN

Every day, commuters all over the world rush to catch trains to get to work as quickly as possible. In Sweden's capital city, however, there is one metro train that you would be very happy to miss.

Back in the 1960s, the authorities decided to try out a new train for Stockholm's metro. Unlike the existing trains, which were painted green, this eight-car train was unadorned, a shiny metallic aluminium. This made it impossible to miss and it seemed to glow as it rushed through the underground tunnels. The locals called it the Silverpilen, or Silver Arrow.

Almost immediately, stories began to develop about this unusual train. By the 1970s it was legendary, and not in a good way. Some said that once you stepped on board the Silver Arrow, it was impossible to get off. Time seemed to stand still once you were inside and although you may have wanted to travel only one stop, you could find yourself sitting there for a week before you were finally let off at some random destination. Many girls refused to board the ghost train, for fear of where they would end up. This ghostly train was also apparently seen hurtling through tunnels and stations in the middle of the night, long after the metro had closed.

As the metro network was expanded, a new station was built at a place called Kymlinge, which had been earmarked for

LEFT
Today, Kymlinge Station is a deserted and desolate place, where trains rush past without stopping

economic development. Kymlinge was an eerie place. As it was not yet in use, the platforms had no signs and no colourful notices or advertisements. It seemed very much like a ghost station.

In the end, the development was shelved and Kymlinge station never opened to passengers or trains – except perhaps to the Silver Arrow. The story goes that this ghostly train would stop only there, to pick up and set down its passengers from among the living dead. Anyone living who was unlucky enough to get on this ghostly train headed towards Kymlinge would never be seen again.

ABOVE It is said that anyone who accidentally boards the Silver Arrow is never seen again

ABOVE This photograph from 1936, of the Brown Lady of Raynham Hall, is one of the most famous images of a ghost of all time

INSET King George IV was certain he had seen the ghost when he stayed in the house, and equally certain he did not wish to spend another night there

THE LADY IN BROWN

It is not often that a ghostly apparition is definitively captured on film, but that is precisely what happened at Raynham Hall in Norfolk. For many people, this has laid to rest once and for all any doubts they may have had about the existence of ghosts.

In the 18th century, Raynham Hall was the home of Viscount Charles Townshend and his second wife, Dorothy Walpole. They were married in 1713, but when Charles discovered that his wife had had a relationship before their marriage, with a notorious philanderer, he was absolutely furious. He kept Dorothy a virtual prisoner at Raynham Hall and even forbade her from seeing their own children. At the age of 40, she died. The official story was that she contracted smallpox, but others said that Charles pushed her down the grand central staircase.

Ever since then, people have reported seeing a ghostly figure wearing a dress of brown brocade. Sometimes she carries a lamp and her empty black eye sockets are utterly terrifying. King George IV, no less, reported being woken by her spirit while staying at Raynham, whereupon he promptly left the house. In 1926, the current Marquis Townshend saw a brown figure on the stairs, and recognised it from the portrait of Lady Dorothy that hung in the house. According to members of the royal household, Queen Elizabeth II herself saw the ghostly visitor when she was a guest at Raynham and whatever it was made her corgis bark uncontrollably.

In 1936, the magazine *Country Life* was preparing a feature on the historic interiors of the house. Photographers Indre Shira and Hubert Provand were about to finish for the day when Shira was aghast to see a spectral figure descending the staircase. Calmly, he told Provand to take a picture. What emerged was truly astonishing, for there, without a doubt, was the luminous figure of a woman in a long dress descending the stairs. Some sceptics have said the figure resembles a statue of the Virgin Mary and the image is the result of a double exposure, an elaborate hoax, but others are convinced this is proof that this troubled spirit continues to haunt the house where she was so miserably to spend, and end, her life.

ABOVE Today the headquarters of Coutts Bank are in an impressive, modern building in London

THE DUKE OF NORFOLK AT COUTTS

Coutts is one of the most prestigious private banking houses in Britain. Its handsome headquarters on The Strand in London have, however, been the setting for troubled happenings.

Its history dates back centuries and it has managed the accounts of numerous important clients, including Queen Elizabeth II. However, in the early 1990s, staff in the building began to notice some strange goings-on. Lights in the office would switch on and off without warning and their computer screens flickered. They thought some electrical surge was probably to blame – until they saw a ghostly figure in black walk calmly past them. To make their terrifying experience even more paralysing, this figure appeared to have no head. When staff started refusing to

come to work because they were too scared of what they might see, the bank was forced to act. Extraordinarily, they called on the services of the College of Psychic Studies to investigate. The College sent along a medium called Eddie Burks. Eddie's day job was as a civil engineer, but he had discovered he also had a gift for spiritual healing. Having interviewed the staff, he held a séance in the building at which, to everyone's amazement, he made contact with the spirit of an aristocratic man from history. This was Thomas Howard, 4th Duke of Norfolk, who had been

found guilty of plotting against Queen Elizabeth I and executed at a location near the building, in 1572. He was a Catholic and vehemently opposed to the Protestant faith being imposed by the Queen. The Coutts building was not there in the 16th century, but it seemed the Duke's spirit had become trapped in its walls. The spirit apparently told Burks he was bitter and tortured and longed to be released to find peace.

Burks is said to have raised up the spirit of the Duke's daughter, who appeared to him in a dazzle of white light. She took hold of her father's hand and led him away, so that together they could find peace at last. No more sightings of the Duke at Coutts have been reported since.

✝✝✝✝

RIGHT Thomas Howard, 4th Duke of Norfolk, was executed nearby in 1572. Was it his ghostly presence that disturbed the offices and computers (inset) of Coutts employees?

THE PHANTOM HITCHHIKER

Today, hitchhikers are not a common sight, but a few decades ago it was quite usual to see young people standing by the side of the road, thumbs held up, hoping for a free ride. Some drivers who picked up these strangers got far more than they bargained for.

A young man was driving one night when he saw a young woman standing by the side of the road, looking cold. He pulled up beside her, opened the door and let her in. She looked so chilled that he offered her his white jumper to help her warm up. She told him her car had swerved off the road and she needed to get back to her parents' house. It was then that he noticed that her face and hands were covered in scratches. They drove for a few miles, to the end of a lane, where there was a house whose lights were shining out into the night. This was the place, she told him, as she got out of the car, thanking him.

A few days later, the driver remembered that the girl had left wearing his jumper. He retraced his journey and found the lane leading up to her parents' house. Knocking on the door, he was met by an elderly couple. They invited him in, and there on a shelf was a photograph of the young woman he had met a few days earlier. He was astonished to hear that their 19-year-old daughter had been killed 40 years ago, in a car accident on her way home one night.

LEFT
An unfinished journey compelled one spirit to ask for help

The young man could not believe that his passenger had not been a living, breathing person. She had seemed so very real. As he drove slowly passed the nearby cemetery, however, his eye was caught by something flapping in the wind. He felt compelled to stop the car, get out and investigate; as he approached the object, he was appalled to realise that this was his jumper, the one he had given to his chilly passenger. It was draped over the headstone of a 19-year-old local girl, who had tragically died 40 years before.

ABOVE Ghost stories often have links to graveyards. Do the spirits feel a close connection to the place they are laid to rest?

INTERESTING FACT

VANISHING HITCHHIKER STORIES ARE SAID TO PREDICT FUTURE EVENTS, INCLUDING NATURAL DISASTERS AND THE END OF A WAR.

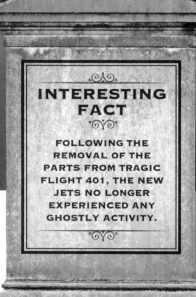

INTERESTING FACT

FOLLOWING THE REMOVAL OF THE PARTS FROM TRAGIC FLIGHT 401, THE NEW JETS NO LONGER EXPERIENCED ANY GHOSTLY ACTIVITY.

ABOVE Some believe that ghosts that warn of danger are good spirits, or angels

INSET Airline professionals take their responsibilities to their passengers extremely seriously – sometimes apparently even from beyond the grave

FLIGHT ⊕①①① TO MIAMI

Most people feel a little anxiety before a flight, hoping that they will reach their destination safely. Thankfully, this is almost always the case. Just occasionally, accidents do occur and there is one story of an airplane accident that has a truly ghostly ending.

It was 1972 and Eastern Airlines flight 401 was heading for Miami, Florida. On board were 163 passengers and 13 crew members. As the pilots prepared to land, not all the indicator lights showed that the wheels were down. As they struggled to check what was happening, the autopilot switched itself off and the plane began rapidly losing altitude. Tragically, the plane crashed into the Florida Everglades. First Officer Stockstill died immediately; Captain Loft and Flight Engineer Repo survived, but later died of their injuries. Many passengers were also killed.

Some valuable parts of the plane were in a good enough state to be reused in other aircraft, and this is where the troubles began. When the Vice President of the airline boarded one of these aircraft before everyone else, he was surprised to find a Captain sitting up in first class. As he sat down for a chat with him, he froze. This was none other than Captain Loft from Flight 401 – who quickly disappeared. Soon after this, another captain was checking the instruments before a flight when he saw Engineer Repo sitting beside him. He heard him say, as clear as day, 'There will never be another crash on an L1011. We will not let it happen.' Several caterers saw him, too, and two passengers even called a flight attendant when the uniformed officer sitting next to them seemed unresponsive – hardly surprising as this figure of Repo then vanished into thin air.

One final incident changed everything. Several stewardesses on Flight 903 to Mexico City saw the face of Repo appear in the door of one of their ovens. When it spoke, it said, 'Watch out for fire on this plane.' The flight landed safely, but on the way back to New York one of its engines caught fire and failed. Thankfully no one was hurt and the plane landed, but the crew were severely shaken. It was time for Eastern Airlines to act. All the salvaged parts from Flight 401 were removed from the jets that had experienced these unsettling hauntings.

CAPE OF GOOD HOPE
THE MOST SOUTH—WESTERN POINT
OF THE AFRICAN CONTINENT

ABOVE The stormy seas off the Cape of Good Hope
make it a notoriously dangerous place for ships

THE FLYING DUTCHMAN

The Flying Dutchman is the most well known of ghost ships, doomed to sail the oceans forever and for any sailors unfortunate enough to catch sight of her, a sure sign that tragedy is waiting just over the next wave.

In 1680, Captain Hendrick van der Decken set sail with his crew on a voyage from Amsterdam to Batavia, a port in Dutch East India. As the ship rounded the Cape of Good Hope, a violent storm came up. The captain tried desperately to keep his ship afloat and it seems they nearly made it, but eventually the storm got the better of the vessel and it foundered and sank. All lives on board were lost.

The story goes that, as he wrestled with his ship amid the towering waves, van der Decken screamed out, 'I will round this Cape even if I have to keep sailing until doomsday!'

The captain's last words seemed to have come true and *The Flying Dutchman* is destined to sail the oceans for all eternity. If it is hailed by another ship, it is said, the sailors on board will try to send messages back to land, to people who are long dead. The ship has been sighted many times, including by royalty. In 1880, Prince George of Wales, the future King George V, was on a three-year voyage with his elder brother Prince Albert and their tutor. On the 11th July 1881, off the coast of Australia, he recorded in the ship's log '...a strange red light as of a phantom ship all aglow, in the midst of which the masts, spars and sails of a brig 200 yards distant stood out in strong relief as she came up on the port bow ... on arriving there was no vestige nor any sign whatever of any material ship to be seen... 13 persons altogether saw her ... the ordinary seaman who had this morning reported *The Flying Dutchman* fell from the foretopmast crosstrees on to the topgallant forecastle and was smashed to atoms.'

The most recent recorded sighting of this ghostly vessel was in 1942, off the coast of Cape Town in South Africa. Four witnesses clearly saw *The Flying Dutchman* sail into Table Bay – and vanish into thin air.

INSET *The Flying Dutchman* has been sighted at sea by sailors for centuries since it sank beneath the waves

RIGHT The Cape of Good Hope is sometimes dubbed the Cape of Storms. It is a rocky headland on the Atlantic coast of the Cape Peninsula, South Africa

POSTBRIDGE ROAD, DARTMOOR

Sometimes, Dartmoor can be a desolate place. It is no surprise to anyone who has the misfortune to be passing across the moor at night, or in fog, that it is one of the most haunted places in Britain.

The road across Dartmoor, in Devon, passes between two settlements, first Postbridge and then Two Bridges. During the 20th century, the section of road between these two places was the scene of some seriously scary goings-on. In each case, drivers reported that the steering wheel of their car seemed to be pulled to one side, making them swerve, and even sometimes crash. This also happened to cyclists and motorcyclists, who were similarly derailed by a tugging on their handlebars.

In the early 1920s, a sinister development began. An army captain, travelling the road on his motorbike, felt a pair of invisible hands grab him and push him over. When he stood up, there was no one there. Shortly after, a young woman called Florence Warwick felt her whole car vibrate. When she stopped to compose herself, she was horrified to see a huge pair of hairy hands pressed against her windscreen. The vision vanished as she screamed and somehow she drove herself on and out of danger.

The local authority tried to reduce the number of incidents on this stretch of road by making repairs, but to no avail. The ghoulish experiences continued.

LEFT
The ghostly hands have terrified several motorists driving over Dartmoor

A couple in a caravan decided to stop there for the night, because a dense fog had suddenly descended on the moor. The wife was woken by a scratching noise. As she sat up she felt an eerie chill surround her and she looked up to see the very same horrible hands at the window. Petrified, she made the sign of a cross on the glass, whereupon the hands disappeared.

No one has ever proposed an explanation for these terrible experiences, beyond mentioning the locals' belief that this stretch of road has long been cursed by a spirit, who met his end in this remote spot and has ever since been seeking other souls to join him.

ABOVE Dartmoor is bleak and wildly beautiful, but not a place to linger after the sun goes down

INTERESTING FACT

DARTMOOR IS ALSO SAID TO BE HAUNTED BY A CLOAKED FIGURE THAT STANDS BY BEETOR CROSS, ITS EMPTY EYE SOCKETS WATCHING THE ROAD AHEAD.

INTERESTING FACT

ACTRESS JUDI DENCH REPORTED SEEING THE GHOST OF JOHN BALDWIN BUCKSTONE AT THE HAYMARKET THEATRE IN LONDON.

INSET The Theatre Royal, Drury Lane has a gruesome past, but a friendly ghost

ABOVE A man in Victorian dress has been spotted at the Haymarket Theatre by some of it's famous guests

THEATRICAL GHOSTS OF LONDON

Everyone enjoys going to the theatre to be scared by a great thriller, but when the curtain comes down, we expect the frights to end. In London's Drury Lane theatre, however, some people have experienced terrors beyond the stage.

The Theatre Royal in Drury Lane has a very long history. The theatre standing there today was built in 1812, but it is the fourth building to have been constructed on the site, which first hosted a theatre in 1663, when Charles II granted it a royal charter. Over the centuries, no doubt many nefarious practices have taken place within its walls and several spirits seem to be reluctant to leave. The most famous ghost is the Man in Grey, a gentleman in 18th-century dress of a grey suit, powdered wig, riding boots, tricorn hat – and sword. This elegant character has often been seen wandering through the dress circle during rehearsals, before vanishing through the walls. The actors and crew of Drury Lane are quite unfazed by their guest, indeed his appearance is taken as an omen of good luck for a production or a performance.

Although the current building dates from the 19th century, the areas below the stage are much, much older. Down here it is difficult not to be spooked by feelings of eerie presences from long ago. It was down here, in 1848, that builders renovating the theatre found a bricked-up side passage. On opening it they were horrified to find a human skeleton – with a dagger still stuck between its ribs. Could this have been the fate of the troubled Man in Grey?

Other ghosts are said to lurk amid London's Haymarket Theatre. John Baldwin Buckstone was the theatre's actor-manager for decades during the 19th century and obviously had a deep affection for it. So deep, in fact, that he finds it hard to leave. In 2009, Patrick Stewart told his fellow actors that he saw Buckstone standing in the wings as he came off stage for the interval in a production of *Waiting for Godot*. He is by no means the first to see him; several others have reported seeing him standing watching the performers in his Victorian frock coat.

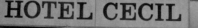

ELISA LAM

ABOVE The Hotel Cecil in Los Angeles was the location for the utterly mysterious disappearance of a young woman

Sometimes a modern ghost story comes to light that makes us realise that the paranormal is just as likely to happen in our world today as in the past. The unfathomable strangeness of the story of Elisa Lam is enough to give anyone nightmares.

Elisa Lam was a 21-year-old Canadian student, studying in Vancouver. In 2013, she set out alone on a tour around a series of cities on the west coast of the United States. On the 26th January she arrived in Los Angeles and checked in to the Hotel Cecil. Every day, Elisa would call her parents back home, so when she didn't call they were worried and reported her missing to the LA police. Initial searches found nothing, but after three weeks guests in the hotel started complaining about the quality of their water. Finally, Elisa was found. Her naked body was floating in a water tank on the building's roof. The door to the roof was locked and alarmed and the tank had a very heavy lid, plus it was securely fastened. How could Elisa possibly have got up here and why would she have done so?

The hotel is apparently known for incidents of paranormal activity. On the day of her disappearance, Elisa used one of the lifts. An extraordinary video from a CCTV camera inside the lift gives some idea of what may have been happening on her last day. She gets in the lift, presses all the buttons, then gets out again, waving her arms around as if warding off an unseen attacker, although the corridor is clearly empty. She gets in the lift again, appearing to hide, then exits once more. What was she so afraid of? Her strange behaviour carries on for several minutes, before Elisa finally leaves the lift for the last time.

The mystery of Elisa's death has never been resolved, but the peculiar behaviour shown in the elevator has prompted many to think that this poor girl may have been guided by an unseen force that led to her tragic end.

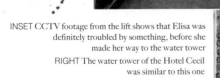

INSET CCTV footage from the lift shows that Elisa was definitely troubled by something, before she made her way to the water tower
RIGHT The water tower of the Hotel Cecil was similar to this one

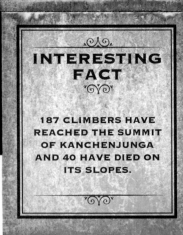

ABOVE Scaling Kanchenjunga is a formidable challenge for any climber and for Wanda Rutkiewicz it was, tragically, a trial too far. Although she never returned, it seems she did want to make one last call (inset) to her old friend

CALL ME

In the modern world, where so much of our lives is run by technology, it's easy to think that there is no place for the supernatural. Yet there are plenty of examples of spirits trying to cross the divide between the dead and the living, using the most up-to-date means available. This story is one of thousands of people hearing from lost loved ones on the phone.

In 1986, Wanda Rutkiewicz, an accomplished Polish mountaineer, became the first woman ever to climb K2, the second highest mountain in the world after Everest, and also in the Himalayas. This was an amazing achievement and she followed it with more mountaineering marvels, determined as she was to conquer all 14 of the 2,440 m (8,000 ft) peaks. In 1992, she set her sights on climbing Kanchenjunga, the world's third highest mountain and her ninth peak, once again in that most challenging of ranges, the Himalayas. This time, tragically, Rutkiewicz's luck ran out. Sheltering at high altitude on the north-west face, she was last seen by fellow mountaineer Carlos Carsolio. He tried to persuade her to descend, but she refused. She was weakened and confused by the cold, he said, and unable to make a rational decision.

Rutkiewicz never returned from Kanchenjunga and her body was never recovered. Her friends and family mourned her loss, but it was not long before her friend Ewa Matuszewska was woken in the night by the telephone ringing. Answering it, she clearly heard Wanda's voice. Ewa was so happy to hear from her friend and, hoping beyond hope that she had found a way down the mountain after all, asked her, 'Where are you? We are all in despair.' The voice replied, 'I am cold, I am very cold, but don't cry. Everything will be fine.' Ewa wanted to know more. 'Why aren't you coming back?' she asked. Stricken, she heard her friend reply, 'I cannot now,' before the line went dead.

THE FACEBOOK GHOST

Facebook links millions of people around the world, in ways no one would have thought possible a few decades ago. It's great to be able to keep in touch with friends at the tap of a screen or click of a mouse – but nobody expects that connection to last beyond the grave.

Nathan and Emily were a happy young couple starting out on life together as boyfriend and girlfriend, until the day that Emily's life was tragically cut short in a car crash in 2012. In 2014, Nathan posted the following story on Reddit. He had left Emily's Facebook account open as it felt too final, and too painful, to close it. Then in September 2013, he received a message from Emily. Only Emily's mother had her login and password details, so he checked she was not responsible for this message out of the blue. The message seemed to be recycling old messages from their shared chat history, so Nathan assumed it must be some tech-savvy hacker messing around. He changed the login and password details and hoped it would stop. Soon, however, Emily began tagging herself in Nathan's new photos. Her friends thought Nathan was responsible for this sick joke and many unfriended him.

Still the messages continued, using recycled words and phrases from their old conversations. Then one day the first original word arrived: 'FREEZING'. This gave poor Nathan serious nightmares. In the horrific car accident, Emily's body had been crushed and one of her legs had been severed. A couple of months later, a new message arrived: 'Just let me walk.' This was followed by the rewriting of the messages Nathan had sent her on the day she died, asking frantically where she was and asking her to call him. Now Nathan decided finally to memorialise Emily's Facebook page, in the hope of bringing his ordeal to an end.

LEFT
Social media is the ultimate modern location for a haunting

The final alert he received from Facebook was of a photo that she had once posted – of his front door and his computer, taken from outside his house.

Commentators online have reacted in a variety of ways to Nathan's story. Some believe it, others do not. Who knows the truth behind this most modern, tragic tale?

✝✝✝✝✝

ABOVE A car accident tragically cut short Emily's life, but did she really try to reach out to Nathan from beyond the grave?

INTERESTING FACT

FACEBOOK HAS MORE THEN TWO BILLION USERS AND IS VIEWED ON EVERY CONTINENT OF EARTH.

ANGELS AND DEMONS

In many cases of ghostly presences, the visitors seem benign, as if they have come to offer protection. We often think of these as our guardian angels. Demons, on the other hand, have quite a different agenda.

Some of the most uplifting stories of the unexplained are ones that people see as being in some way miraculous. Prayers are answered or disaster is averted. Sometimes, lives are even saved. Early in the 20th century, in the Netherlands, a lay preacher called Breet was approached by a man who had come to offer him a confession. That confession turned out to relate to Breet himself. The man told him how, some years earlier, he and a friend had been sent to kill Breet. They had lured him out of his house and waited in the shadowy street to attack him and drown him in a nearby canal. Their plan was foiled, however, when they spotted two companions on either side of the preacher. They could not overpower three men, and had to let him go. Breet remembered the day very well, but he assured them he had been quite alone in the street. His only explanation: 'The Lord must have sent two angels to keep me safe.'

Demons, on the other hand, feature in many people's worst nightmares. These are spirits that haunt with malice. They want to cause trouble, even death, and they will go so far as to attempt to possess a living person to achieve their ambitions. However, we have far fewer examples of demonic activity than we do of angels coming to our aid. Why might this be? The word 'demon' comes from the Greek daemon, which simply means spirit or deity. Although our history is full of acts of what could be called evil, we can usually find a cause for these in our all-too human nature. Perhaps demons are little more than us expressing our worst fears of what we are capable of.

RIGHT The common image of a demon is terrifying, but stories of demons are very rare
INSET It is comforting to think of guardian angels looking out for us

HELPFUL GHOSTS

It is remarkable how often people report the emergence of a helpful figure in a time of need. Someone who vanishes without trace, having saved them from trouble. Humans are capable of acts of kindness, but sometimes a story comes along that seems impossible to explain rationally.

In 1983, William Porter and his wife were visiting his parents in California with their toddler daughter, Helen. While talking with the adults inside, they heard Helen cry out from the garden. Rushing outside, they saw her standing on the path near the fish pond, soaking wet and very upset. The pool was at least 1.2 m (4 ft) deep and Helen, aged two, could not swim. She had fallen in, but she could not possibly have got herself out of it alone. Strangely, there were no wet footprints or puddles on the 6 m (20 ft) stretch of flagstones between Helen and the pond – just the puddle she was standing in, screaming. When her anxious parents asked her what had happened, she told them of a man dressed all in white who had pulled her straight out of the water – then disappeared.

Another story relates to a job where the pressures can be very great and the outcome of making mistakes severe. Ruby was working as a nurse on a busy ward. She was newly trained and feeling distinctly out of her depth. One night, an older nurse came up to her and asked her to check on the patient in room eight.

Ruby duly went to check and found the woman in trouble. Luckily, Ruby was able to help her in time and all was well. As the shift progressed through the night, Ruby found her colleague offering advice again and again, guiding her to those most in need. Her patients remarked, too, on the elderly nurse who had visited them.

LEFT Can spirits help us in our time of need?

In the morning, when the new shift came on duty, Ruby told them about the woman she had shared her night with. That's when they told her that she had been alone on the ward. But Ruby was not the first, they said, to report the presence of this helpful nurse. Martha was well known for offering her aid to newly qualified nurses and their patients – 30 years after her own death.

†‡‡†

ABOVE When Ruby was feeling scared and out her depth, an elderly angel came to her aid

INTERESTING FACT

MANY PEOPLE BELIEVE THAT EVERYONE HAS A GUARDIAN ANGEL AND THAT ARCHANGELS SUPERVISE ALL OF THE GUARDIAN ANGELS ON EARTH.

ABOVE The charge of the Ninth Lancers during the 'Great Retreat' from Mons to Cambrai is shown here attacking a German battery in August 1914

INSET Conditions for the soldiers fighting in World War I were truly terrible, they needed all the help they could get

THE ANGELS OF MONS

World War I was the bloodiest and most terrible in modern history. Given the terrible loss of life, and the appalling conditions that the soldiers were forced to endure in the trenches and on the battlefield, it is hardly surprising that stories of ghostly spirits began to circulate.

For some, it became commonplace to see the ghosts of their recently living comrades alongside them in their time of horror. There is one story, however, that gained such support that it is still spoken of today. In August 1914, the war was going badly for the British army. They were entrenched in northern France, attempting to hold back the rapidly advancing German army. They were massively outnumbered, but on the morning of the 22nd August were ordered to advance against the enemy. Seeing the impossibility of their situation, and having suffered heavy casualties, the British were eventually forced to retreat. This war was going to be harder to win than everyone had initially thought. In September, a writer back in London published a story called *The Bowmen*, apparently a first-hand account of how the soldiers had been saved from complete destruction by a host of ghostly bowmen, the reincarnation of Henry V's archers from the Battle of Agincourt of 1415

These miraculous saviours appeared in a shining golden light on the battlefield and were summoned by a soldier calling out to St George, the patron saint of England, to come to their aid in their time of need.

Soon the story was being published in parish magazines all over England. In some places it was changed slightly, as several officers and soldiers spoke instead of a host of angels, rather than archers, that had appeared in the midst of this appalling scene. By Christmas 1914, the legend of The Angels of Mons had taken root across the country. These angelic warriors protected the British soldiers from the worst of the German attack, allowing them to retreat. To think of divine intervention on the side of the Allies was certainly good for morale, at home and on the battlefield, and that is just what was needed at this point in the war.

PHANTOM WRITERS AND PAINTERS

It seems reasonable to believe that ghosts appear because they want to communicate with the living. They want us to know that they are not at peace. Sometimes, they communicate through writing and painting.

The spiritual practice of automatic writing is also known as psychography. A living person feels taken over by a spirit, who guides their mouth into speaking or their hand into writing messages that come from an unseen place. Back in the 1960s, an American poet called Jane Roberts began to receive messages. As she sat in a trance-like state, they were spoken to her by an entity who called himself Seth. As she heard them she repeated his words out loud, so they could be written down by her husband. Seth described himself as 'an energy personality essence no longer focused in physical matter', which sounds like a good definition of a ghost. This extraordinary flow of communication carried on unbroken for many years, until Jane finally died, in 1984. The body of writing that resulted, the *Seth Material*, became internationally famous. After each session, Jane claimed not to remember what Seth had said through her. Seth discussed some pretty big questions, such as the nature of physical reality, the nature of good and evil and of God, the origins of the universe and all aspects of death and rebirth.

Others have felt compelled to make marks by spirits communicating through them from beyond the grave. In the 19th century, in a dimly lit English parlour, a woman called Georgiana Houghton was overtaken by a series of spirit guides. These invisible forces guided her hand to produce a series of extraordinarily vibrant and colourful abstract paintings. These, she claimed, had been sent to her by various people, including the spirits of Titian and Correggio, famous Italian artists of the 16th century. The amazing thing was that, at that time, abstract art was completely unknown. Houghton was a genuine pioneer. She produced hundreds of works of art in this trance-like state.

INSET Georgiana Houghton (centre) produced colourful, abstract works of art that she said were imparted to her hand by spirit guides

RIGHT The activity in the brain changes significantly when someone is in a trance-like state, practising psychography

POSSESSION

While some people have felt compelled to write or paint while spirits channel them from the other side, others have felt completely taken over by them – and not always in a good way.

In 1981, a man called Arne Cheyenne Johnson murdered his landlord, Alan Bono, in Connecticut, in the US. The startling thing about the case was that Johnson claimed he was innocent of the crime because he had been possessed by an evil spirit, a demon, who had compelled him to commit the murder. This was the first time in US legal history that demonic possession had been cited as a defence for murder, but what was the story?

Extraordinarily, the demon had first taken over a child, David Glatzel. Over several terrifying weeks, the boy received unexplained scratches and bruises, growled, hissed and talked in otherworldly voices. His desperate parents then called in a series of priests to perform an exorcism and at one of those sessions a demon was seen to fly from David's body and take up residence with Johnson, who was a family friend. Johnson showed all the signs of possession that had afflicted David and finally murdered his landlord in an argument.

The judge dismissed his claim, but Johnson only served five years of his 10–20 year sentence.

A kinder story of possession involved two little girls, both called Mary, back in the 1870s, in Illinois. Mary Vennum was 13-years-old when she began falling into a trance. On being questioned by a doctor, Mary claimed to see the spirit of a Mary Roff, a local girl who had died when Mary Vennum was one year old.

When Mary announced she was going 'home', to the Roff household, her parents bravely let her go. Witnesses were then amazed to see Mary greet her old relatives and call her Sunday School teacher by her maiden name.

LEFT
Possession has been blamed for some terrible crimes, but is it demons, or psychiatric illness?

She was familiar with objects around the house and could remember details of past family holidays and other events. She announced that Mary Roff would soon return to the spirit world and that is exactly what happened. Having said her goodbyes to the family she had left in the land of the living, Mary Roff finally left Mary Vennum in peace.

ABOVE Historically, possession may have been used to explain mysterious illness such as epilepsy or misunderstood mental illnesses, resulting in poor treatment of those already suffering

INTERESTING FACT

WHEN MARY VENNUM LATER MARRIED, THE SPIRIT OF MARY ROFF INHABITED HER TO ALLOW HER TO EXPERIENCE A PAIN-FREE CHILDBIRTH.

ABOVE When demon possession appears to have taken hold, the victim's family usually calls in a priest (inset) to perform an exorcism

EXORCISM

In the creepy case of Robbie Mannheim, his parents were so concerned that their son had been possessed by a demon that they called in exorcists to drive the spirit out. Usually, priests call upon the evil spirit to let go their hold on the living and return to the land of the dead.

A child, known as Robbie Mannheim, was 14 years old in 1949 and living in a suburb of Washington, DC, in the US. He was very close to his aunt Harriet, who had introduced him to the idea of the spirit world, so when she died he was very upset and he tried to communicate with her spirit. This, the story goes, was the point at which a malevolent spirit took possession of him. Marks began to appear on his body and objects near him moved of their own accord. Eventually Robbie's parents called in a Lutheran priest to perform an exorcism. When this was unsuccessful, a second exorcism was tried by an Anglican priest. This, too, failed. When the words 'St Louis' appeared scratched into Robbie's chest, everyone was terrified. This was where aunt Harriet had died. Robbie was moved there and that was where a Catholic priest, Father William Bowdern, faced his greatest ever challenge.

During the exorcism, Robbie spat at Father Bowdern and his bed rocked uncontrollably, while objects flew around the room. In total, the exorcism ritual to cast out demons from Robbie's body was performed 30 times, over a period of two months.

Eventually, Robbie apparently spoke the words 'Christ, Lord' and a great sound like thunder resounded through the building. Robbie then calmly opened his eyes and said simply, 'It's over.'

Robbie's case became famous when it was published as a bestselling book, *The Exorcist*, which was made into a blockbuster film in 1973. Astonishingly, however, once his ordeal was over Robbie never had any memory of his terrifying possession. His identity was kept secret, and he lived a normal, happy life.

TALKING TO THE DEAD

Ghostly apparitions usually appear when people least expect them.
They walk through walls ahead of them in haunted houses or wander
across their path gardens in the evening light. These unnerving
experiences are not consciously chosen, but sometimes people can
consciously want to communicate with spirits on 'the other side'.

If you have lost a loved one, it is natural
to want to hear from them again, to know
they are at peace and perhaps that they
are looking out for you in your life. Many
people find that the best way to contact
these spirits is through a medium. These
individuals propose to act as channels
between the living and the dead, as they
are psychically attuned to receive
messages from the spirit world and
pass them on. Some people are highly
sceptical about mediums, believing
them to be con artists who exploit the
suffering of the bereaved. It is true that
this has become big business and, as
with any other business, some people are
better at it than others. However, there
are so many stories of mediums genuinely
relating information back from one
world to another, that it is difficult
to dismiss them altogether.

Jill Nash has been a medium for many years. She has described one particularly memorable session, when an elderly lady came to see her. As the woman entered the room, Jill saw behind her the figure of an old man, who stood behind her chair as she sat down. Jill instinctively knew this was the woman's husband, who had recently died, and she felt he wanted to tell her about a rose. She passed this on to the elderly lady. As it happened, he had been trying to breed a new kind of rose when he died and he wanted his widow to keep going with the work, as he was sure it would succeed. Jill described the setting for his work with the roses in such detail that the lady was convinced her husband was present. She felt a great sense of comfort.

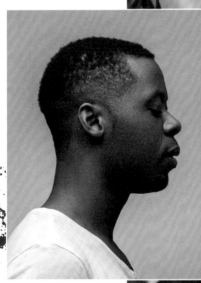

INSET and RIGHT A medium uses extrasensory perception to uncover and relay information from those who have died, such as about the elderly lady's roses (right), which they could not otherwise have known

PSYCHICS AND SENSITIVES

What does it mean to be psychic? Psychics say that almost all of us experience strange examples of intuition regularly, it is just that we choose to ignore these opportunities for developing our psychic understanding. For professional psychics, their powers are too great to ignore.

Psychics often call themselves 'sensitives' because they say that they are particularly sensitive to energy, by which they mean the kind of energy that is given off by all things in the world. Psychics describe their power as being able to harness this energy to know something without any logical connection or thought process. It may be a vibration they feel, a voice they hear or an image that comes to them unbidden. There are many different kinds of psychic ability and most psychics find they have only one or two particular gifts, rather than all of them.

Mediumship is the ability to communicate with the spirit world, of those who have passed away. Mediums may be able to channel messages from these spirits to the living, often to the dead person's relatives and other loved ones. Mediums often relay messages from 'the other side' through the agency of a spirit guide, an entity who claims to have lived on Earth and acquired certain skills, knowledge and wisdom before they died. The obvious question is, is this entity really a separate spirit guide, or is it the voice of the medium's subconscious?

LEFT
Levitation is a rare skill that only very few psychics can perform

ABOVE For centuries, fortune tellers have claimed to have psychic powers that allow them to see the future

In recent decades, channelling has become a more popular name for mediumship.

Telekinesis is another psychic power, the ability to move objects using the power of the mind alone. Precognition allows psychics to foresee events before they happen, either in dreams or in waking visions. Levitation skills involve being able to hover as if weightless above the ground, though this is a very rare skill.

INTERESTING FACT

CRYSTAL BALLS HAVE BEEN USED IN DIVINATION FOR OVER 4,000 YEARS. DIVINATION USES SUPERNATURAL POWERS TO UNLOCK THE FUTURE OR THE UNKNOWN.

ABOVE The Ghost Club was founded by academics at Cambridge University.
Today the Ghost Club does not have premises but it is still going strong

THE GHOST CLUB

The Ghost Club is the oldest organisation in the world associated with psychical research. It was founded in 1862 in England and has its roots at Cambridge University, where two fellows began to discuss ghosts and all kinds of psychic phenomena.

Among the early members of the Ghost Club were the great novelists Charles Dickens and Sir Arthur Conan Doyle. Over the years, it has become one of the foremost organisations for investigating hauntings and it is still in business today.

The Club's stated aim was to investigate all forms of paranormal phenomena in a strictly scientific way. Some of its members were sceptics, which added to its credibility. They scrupulously collected evidence, including the written testimony of as many witnesses as possible. Over the past 150 years, it has investigated many of the most famous British hauntings, including Borley Rectory and Glamis Castle.

One good example involved a family in Clapham, London in the 19th century. Mother and son were sitting in the garden when they saw the elder daughter, Ellen, at the far end of the garden. Ellen was supposed to be in Brighton, where her father had sent her to keep her away from an unsuitable young man.

The mother did not want her husband to see that Ellen had returned, so she told her younger daughter, Mary, to run after her. Mary ran after Ellen as she left the garden and crossed the open fields beyond. Catching up with her, she grasped her hand, only to find it as thin as air. Ellen had vanished. Poor Mary returned, terrified to her mother. The next day the family learned that Ellen had thrown herself into the sea and drowned, at the exact hour that she had appeared to her family in London.

LEFT
In 1938, the famous ghost hunter Harry Price presided over a dinner at the Ghost Club

ABOVE Betty Shine was one of thousands of children evacuated
out of London to the countryside during World War II

BETTY SHINE

Britain's most highly respected and influential medium was Betty
Shine, who died in 2002. Her early career was as an opera singer,
but as she grew older she found she was unable to ignore the
overwhelming psychic powers she knew she possessed.

Betty was 10 years old at the break out of
World War II and, like many children,
was evacuated away from London to the
perceived safety of the countryside to
avoid the Blitz. It was here, scared and
alone, that she claims she found comfort
in the ghostly spirits that would wander
in through her bedroom at night and out
through the walls. Her view was always
that we are not purely physical beings,
but that we possess an energy as well,
which is continuously radiating from us.
Psychics believe that they can see this in
the living and after we die it is this
energy that sometimes lingers, which we
perceive as spirits.

Betty Shine certainly had some
extraordinary cases in her long career.
On one occasion, she was asked for help
by a middle-aged woman who had long
felt depressed. As she was standing
beside her, Betty sensed a dark entity
overshadowing the woman and it even
spoke to her, saying, 'I will never leave
her, she is mine.' She began to pray for
protection from this malevolent spirit,
whereupon a bright white light appeared
around it, casting it into silhouette. The
outline of a man was clearly visible and
as he was dragged away Betty heard
a piercing scream. At that point,
the woman covered her ears.

After recovering from the shock, the woman told Betty about the sadistic, controlling first husband she had escaped from in South Africa decades earlier. Enraged, he had followed her to England, and refused to leave her alone, until one day he fell down dead on her doorstep from a heart attack. Although she had remarried, she still felt depressed and plagued by his presence. After her session with Betty, however, the black cloud had finally lifted and she felt free for the first time in decades.

The popular press dubbed Betty Shine 'the world's number one healer'. She had a very down-to-earth approach and accepted that too many mediums are in fact charlatans. She was, however, deeply moved to share her healing abilities and to reassure others that the spirit world need hold no fears for us.

†┼╫┼†

RIGHT Mediums sometimes claim to feel, or even see, the presence of spirits from beyond the grave. It is unclear whether the 'spirit' (top) captured in this photograph was a living person or not

MIRABELLI

In the months and years after the end of World War I, the world was reeling from so much loss of life. With huge numbers of people grieving for loved ones, it is hardly surprising that interest grew in spiritualism, ideas of the afterlife and contacting the dead.

Inevitably, some people exploited this opportunity to make money and set themselves up as mediums, despite being complete fakes. They gave the bereaved false hope and dishonest reports of messages from the dead and greatly damaged the reputation of their profession. There were some mediums, however, whose apparently genuine psychic powers could not be dismissed so easily. One of these was a man called Carlos Mirabelli.

It seemed that Mirabelli's powers were many and various. He would make objects appear out of thin air and move around the room without being touched. At other times he would enter into a trance and would then speak in an extraordinary variety of foreign languages, including German, French, Dutch, Greek, Polish, Syrian, Albanian, Czech, Italian, Arabic, Turkish, Hebrew, Chinese, Japanese and several African dialects. He also produced automatic writing, including long essays, in 28 languages on complex subjects – despite his education having ended with primary school. Teams of doctors, scientists and psychic investigators attended his sessions over the years

and could find no signs of trickery or subterfuge.

Among the most amazing of Mirabelli's powers was his ability to conjure up spirits in the room. At one session, in broad daylight, the spirit of a young girl appeared in front of a room full of witnesses. One of those present, a Dr de Souza, recognised the girl as his daughter, who had recently died of influenza. She was wearing the dress she had been buried in and her tearful father embraced her for a full 30 minutes before she disappeared. He later told how they had discussed details of their family life that only she could have known.

LEFT
Carlos Mirabelli was a Brazilian medium

ABOVE The man with his arms crossed was allegedly conjured up by
Mirabelli before an audience

The book cover held:

NEW YORK TIMES bestselling author and
Co-Executive Producer of *THE GHOST WHISPERER*

JAMES VAN PRAAGH

UNCOVERING THE TRUTH
ABOUT THE OTHER SIDE

ghosts
AMONG US

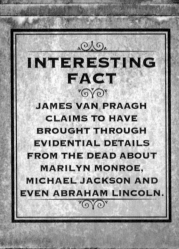

INTERESTING FACT

JAMES VAN PRAAGH
CLAIMS TO HAVE
BROUGHT THROUGH
EVIDENTIAL DETAILS
FROM THE DEAD ABOUT
MARILYN MONROE,
MICHAEL JACKSON AND
EVEN ABRAHAM LINCOLN.

ABOVE For James Van Praagh a clutch of
seven eggs (inset) marked the beginning of an
extraordinary story

JAMES VAN PRAAGH

One of the best-known mediums working in the US today is James Van Praagh. As is often the case, James knew from a very young age that he had special abilities. For many years he tried to ignore them, but eventually he had to confront his skills and put them to use.

When he was a boy on a school trip to a nature reserve, James met another boy who told him his name was Eddie. He was wearing a leg brace and seemed sad and lonely. When James turned away from him, he disappeared. Terrified, he put the experience to the back of his mind. Many years later, in middle age, James was in a supermarket when a boy dropped a carton of eggs at his feet – then vanished into thin air. The name on the carton was clear, 'Mother Hen Nurseries'. Soon after that, James opened his mailbox to find a bird's nest filled with seven eggs. That evening, the same boy appeared to him in his home, his hands tied with rope. When James spoke to him, the boy opened his mouth and spewed out a mouthful of soil.

James was working in a bookshop at that time and shortly after this disturbing incident, he was wrapping a book when it fell open to a page with an illustration called 'The Premature Burial'. Suddenly the penny dropped. Had the boy been telling him he had been buried alive?

Driving home in his car that night, the boy suddenly appeared again, this time sitting beside him, holding the bird's nest in his lap. James pulled over – and saw he was in Bird's Nest Lane. Now he knew he was on to something. Proceeding slowly down the lane, he came to Mother Hen Nurseries. What was more, he realised he had seen this place before; a little further down the lane he came to the nature reserve where, so many years ago, he had met the young child, Eddie.

James left his car and walked through the reserve. Gradually, he felt the spirits of seven boys emerging around him. You can imagine the reception he received when he called the police, but when they finally arrived they unearthed the remains of seven children. Six had their hands bound with rope. The seventh wore a leg brace.

ABOVE At one time, holding a séance was a popular form of evening entertainment

SÉANCES

For many centuries, the idea of talking to the dead was shunned. But in the middle of the 19th century, the idea of summoning the spirits of the dead took thrilling hold of the Victorian imagination and the most popular way to do this was with a séance.

Traditional séances took place in darkened parlours, where a group of people hoping to communicate with the spirit world would sit around a table and hold hands. The spirit medium, the channel through whom the spirits would talk to the living, was in control of the meeting. As they focused their energy on reaching out to the other side, they would fall into a trance. The assembled company watched in awe as they summoned up a spirit guide, a messenger to select the voices that would come through to the living.

The 1860s was a tumultuous time in America, with the Civil War raging.

As Abraham Lincoln led the northern states of the US in the fighting, his wife Mary Lincoln was at home, watching helplessly as their young son Willie died of typhoid fever. Both Willie's parents were distraught in their grief, not least because they had already lost another son, Eddy, who died aged four. Mary turned to spiritualism and to mediums for comfort. She summoned a series of mediums to the Red Room in the White House, in an attempt to make contact with her sons once more. Cranston Laurie and his family were famous mediums of the time and at these séances she did reportedly make contact with the children.

The Lincolns were greatly comforted and Mary claimed often to see the spirits of Willie and Eddy at the foot of her bed.

In modern times, séances are more a form of entertainment. The medium performs his or her art in a theatre, sitting on stage while a large audience is before them and the lights remain on. Still, however, the medium claims to be making contact with the other side and to be channelling messages from the loved ones of people in the audience. Sometimes their fakery is easily apparent, but sometimes the connections they make convince many people present that a bridge has been built to a world beyond death.

INSET Abraham Lincoln is shown here with his family in around the 1860s

RIGHT People visit modern séances in the hope that either the medium can genuinely contact the dead, or to prove the medium is a fake

FAMOUS SÉANCES

As the craze for spiritualism grew and grew in the second half of the 19th century, a number of extraordinary séances took place.

In the 1880s, a medium called Daniel Dunglas Home made his name by performing an extraordinary feat at his séances – he would levitate, or float, off the floor. What's more, he did this not in darkened parlours with shadowy corners, but in well-lit rooms. At one of his séances in 1857, five witnesses reported that Home levitated up to 1.2 m (4 ft) off the ground, while sitting in his chair. One of those present was the novelist, Sir Arthur Conan Doyle, who was also a keen supporter of spiritualism. Home continued to do this for 40 years, attracting the attention of many more influential figures of the time.

The Irish poet WB Yeats was a keen supporter of the paranormal. He was a member of a secret society called the Hermetic Order of the Golden Dawn, devoted to the study of the occult and the paranormal. He was only 20 years old when he attended his first séance, which he clearly found thrilling, and it was not long before he met a medium called Georgie Hyde-Lees. They fell in love and were married and their joint interest in the occult must have led to some powerful séance sessions. One night, Yeats asked his wife to act as medium for him to receive a poem from the other side. He claimed that at the séance a spirit directed his hand to write automatically. He had no knowledge of what flowed from his pen, but at the end of the séance, when he came round, he had written a poem. He added it to his compilation of writings on the occult called *A Vision*.

LEFT
A séance featured in a silent German movie in 1922, *Dr Mabuse: The Gambler*

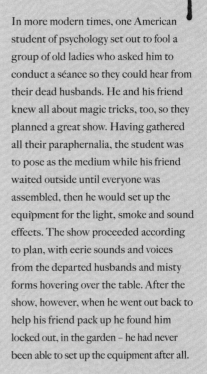

In more modern times, one American student of psychology set out to fool a group of old ladies who asked him to conduct a séance so they could hear from their dead husbands. He and his friend knew all about magic tricks, too, so they planned a great show. Having gathered all their paraphernalia, the student was to pose as the medium while his friend waited outside until everyone was assembled, then he would set up the equipment for the light, smoke and sound effects. The show proceeded according to plan, with eerie sounds and voices from the departed husbands and misty forms hovering over the table. After the show, however, when he went out back to help his friend pack up he found him locked out, in the garden – he had never been able to set up the equipment after all.

ABOVE Sir Arthur Conan Doyle became interested in spiritualism around 1886

INTERESTING FACT

ALTHOUGH SIR ARTHUR CONAN DOYLE IS FAMOUS FOR HIS SHERLOCK HOLMES NOVELS, HE ALSO WROTE AROUND 20 BOOKS ON SPIRITUALISM.

INTERESTING FACT

DURING WORLD WAR I, OUIJA BOARDS WERE SO COMMON THAT ALMOST EVERY HOME IN THE US HAD ONE IN THEIR CUPBOARD.

Talking Board Set

YES **OUIJA** NO
MYSTIFYING ORACLE

ABCDEFGHIJKLM
NOPQRSTUVWXYZ
1234567890
GOOD BYE

ABOVE Ouija boards (inset) were originally sold as games, but it is not a good idea to play with one for fun

OUIJA BOARDS

If you are going to communicate with spirits, you might need a little help to clarify just what they are trying to say. This is where the Ouija board comes in.

The Ouija board, or talking board, is a flat board marked with the letters of the alphabet, the numbers 1–9, the words 'yes' and 'no', 'hello' and 'goodbye', along with various symbols and graphics. Users of the board place their fingers on a small, heart-shaped piece of wood or plastic and this moves around the board to spell out words and messages, as if commanded by a spirit. When it was first introduced, in 1890 in the US, it was intended as a game, but during World War I spiritualists began to use it to communicate with the dead and it has been used that way ever since.

Even experienced, professional users of the board caution against using this powerful tool unwisely. It can, they say, open the door to malevolent spirits and cause a great deal of damage. An experimental rock group called The Mars Volta found this out, to their cost. In 2008, they wrote their new album, *Bedlam in Goliath*, based on their experience of using the Ouija board. Their guitarist, Omar Rodriguez-Lopez, found a board while they were in Jerusalem and the band started to play around with it. Immediately, strange events began to happen; the studio flooded, one of the engineers had a nervous breakdown and tracks disappeared from the computer screen before their eyes. Spooked and scared, the band almost cancelled the album, but in the end they decided to do away with the Ouija board instead. Rodriguez-Lopez buried it in a secret location, somewhere he was sure it would never be found again.

Ouija boards have even been used in court cases. In London in 1994, a man called Stephen Young was on trial for murder. His conviction was, however, overturned when it came to light that four of the jurors had contacted the murder victim using a Ouija board at a séance. The board had told them that Young was guilty. In the end, Young was tried again, with a different jury, and again found guilty.

PARANORMAL PUZZLES

The world of the paranormal is a very strange place. Sometimes, events take place that even the most rational scientists cannot explain. These things, beyond our normal experience of the world, seem to suggest to many the existence of another plane of consciousness or realm that we can only dimly and occasionally perceive.

People with the ability to reach this plane, to break through from the everyday world, are often called clairvoyant. The word means 'seeing clearly', which is just what they do. There are three main kinds of clairvoyance. The first is precognition, which is the ability to predict events before they happen. We have all heard stories of psychics predicting accidents and other disasters. The second is retrocognition, which is when the psychic feels they are experiencing events that have already happened, sometimes long ago. They were not there, yet they can see the events in their mind's eye and recount their experiences in detail, often to match existing records. The third is known as remote viewing, which is where psychics witness contemporary places and events that are taking place beyond their physical environment. They are present, though absent.

It's remarkable that in polls, up to 50 per cent of people in Britain believe they have experienced some kind of psychic insight at some time in their lives. The telephone rang and they knew who it would be or they felt the need to contact a loved one who turned out to be in trouble of some kind. Perhaps we all have some of this talent inside us, but most of us choose not to dwell on it.

For those who embrace the paranormal, who welcome the gifts they seem to have and who enjoy using them to enhance the lives of others, their psychic gifts are not frightening. While fake psychics, mediums and other paranormal professions have become big business, conning the unhappy or gullible, many people accept that there are some individuals who have powers they did not seek, but which they cannot ignore.

RIGHT The human mind is a powerful thing, with powers that many think transcend the body and the physical world around us

PSYCHIC HEALING AND SURGERY

If you had psychic powers, the chances are you would want to use them to do good. It cannot be easy to feel you possess strange gifts that many people do not believe in. To put these powers to good use is, therefore, a rewarding choice.

There are many stories about psychics using their powers for healing those who are suffering or in pain.

Psychic healing involves no medications and no elaborate procedures. The purpose of spiritual healing is to enhance and empower a person's natural ability to achieve a perfect state of balance in body, mind and spirit. The healer acts as a channel for the healing energies in order to help bring this about. It is a two-way process; the healer cannot impose healing, the person must work with them and be willing to change what is ailing them.

Raymond Brown is one of the most famous psychic healers working in Britain and he says he has been healing people for over 40 years. When he works with a patient, he goes into a deep trance. At that point, he says, he connects with his spiritual surgeon, Paul of Tarsus, who lived over 2,000 years ago. Paul provides the healing energy that is delivered through the medium of Raymond. Together they have treated patients with all kinds of ailments in their muscles and joints, as well as stomach pain, infertility and neurological problems.

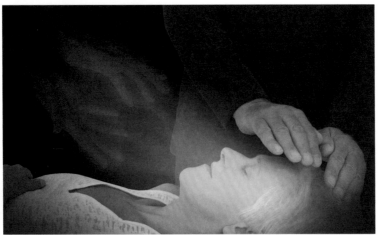

LEFT
Spiritual healers say they channel psychic energy to help their patients

ABOVE People consult a spiritual healer for all kinds of problems. This woman is receiving treatment for her neck pain

These are grand claims, but they are backed up by hundreds of testimonials from down the decades.

Raymond has been filmed by the BBC about his work and in the films Paul speaks through Raymond, saying, 'When I operate, I use instruments which are very similar to those in the physical world. The difference is that you cannot see them. They are spiritual instruments. My hands work through Raymond's and my instruments are inside the patient's body. Patients often tell me they can feel the work going on inside them.'

INTERESTING FACT

ONE OF RAYMOND BROWN'S CLIENTS HAD OSTEOARTHRITIS IN HER KNEE. AFTER THE HEALING SESSIONS, THE KNEE NO LONGER REQUIRED SURGERY.

INTERESTING FACT

BRAZILIAN PSYCHIC JUCELINO NOBREGA DA LUZ PREDICTED THAT FLIGHT JJ3720 WOULD CRASH. THE AIRLINE TOOK HIM SERIOUSLY AND CHANGED THE NUMBER.

ABOVE Many people have claimed to have had a premonition of an impending disaster, such as a plane crash

INSET Visions can be so powerful that people feel they must share them with others

PROPHECY

Prophecy is the foretelling of events before they happen. It has a long and ancient history, but today there are those who believe that their psychic powers give them the ability to predict the future.

Precognition happens when someone actually 'sees' an event that then proceeds to happen at a future time. These spooky paranormal experiences are usually felt as a 'flash' of understanding, a vision, while the visionary is awake. Precognitive experiences usually happen within 24 hours of the future event and unfortunately they mostly concern unhappy events such as accidents, natural disasters and deaths. Intimacy also plays a crucial role. It is more likely that someone will have a vision of an accident or death involving somebody they love or are close to. Of course, visions of natural disasters, such as earthquakes, and major accidents, such as plane crashes, affect many more people.

A man booked on a certain flight, for example, suddenly sees disaster ahead for the aircraft and changes his plans. He watches in horror as the plane he would have caught crashes. Or a mother senses her child is in trouble and hurries to the school playground to find they have had an accident.

Sometimes, precognition comes to those sensitive enough to experience it in their dreams. This can be much harder to capture, to pin down, because we forget our dreams so easily. People with these disturbing skills become expert at remembering and recording their dreams, so they can see their precognition in action.

It may be strange, or it may be quite understandable, but people with the gift of precognition rarely foretell their own deaths. Perhaps the trauma is too great for them to accept it or perhaps they just don't tell. There have been some notable exceptions, however: US President Abraham Lincoln dreamed of his own death six weeks before he was assassinated by a gunman at the theatre. His dream was not of being shot, but of observing the aftermath of his death. He saw a long procession of mourners entering the White House and when he entered himself and passed the coffin, he was shocked to find himself looking at his own body.

DUKE UNIVERSITY EXPERIMENTS

With so much focus on paranormal events in the decades following the tragedy of World War I, it is hardly surprising that many people wanted to try to study these phenomena.

The brand new science of parapsychology was born. One place in the US became the focus of this investigation for a while, Duke University in North Carolina. The driver behind these efforts was Dr JB Rhine, a young academic and former soldier. In the 1930s, he set up the world's first parapsychology laboratory in his department at Duke and, over eight years, conducted an amazing series of tests. What did he think of ghosts and the like? He was not convinced, believing them to be the product of brain tissue using unknown processes to gather and communicate information. Rhine used a set of five cards, each with a simple symbol: a circle, square, star, plus sign or a set of wavy lines. A pack of these was then used to test a person's powers of clairvoyance – going through the pack, they had to predict which symbol would be on the next card to appear, using their special powers. The tester wrote down their answer each time and, over many sets of tests, some people were able to predict more correct answers than the rules of chance would suggest. Did this prove they had some paranormal way of knowing what was on the cards?

As they repeated the experiments multiple times, however, their scores declined. Did this mean they were losing the sharp edge of their psychic ability, as the test lost its novelty value?

Rhine's next experiment looked at a gambler's claim that he could influence the way that dice would fall. This was all about psychokinesis, otherwise known as mind over matter. Could this really be possible? If it could, anyone with serious psychic powers might be able to win a fortune in casinos. Again, Rhine found that his subjects could influence the way the dice fell, but only when their interest was high. His work was criticised for not being rigorous enough, but he was among the first to test and measure this way.

RIGHT and INSET Gamblers could make a fortune if they could predict the fall of the dice or the spin of a roulette wheel

REMOTE VIEWING

Psychics with the power of remote viewing feel they can actually see a place or a thing that is at a remote distance, without using any of their ordinary senses. It's also known as telaesthesia and travelling clairvoyance.

One psychic, Paul Roland, reported his first experience of remote viewing at a meeting of a psychic awareness group. Worrying that he was not receiving visions of the same quality as the others in the room, he asked his host for help. The host rested her hand on his back and invited him to close his eyes. There came into his head a clear picture of an unfamiliar home, complete with a statue of Eros in the garden, which he proceeded to describe in detail. After the session, the host told him he had perfectly described her mother's home in New York. And the statue of Eros? She had been talking to her mother about visiting Piccadilly Circus on her next visit to London, and at the centre of that open space stands, of course, the famous statue of Eros.

This projecting of the consciousness to a distant location is apparently not all that uncommon among psychics. Imagine how useful it could be for a person in one place to be able to visualise a remote location without even going there. That kind of skill sounds like the stuff of fantasy espionage novels. Presumably, the US government felt the same way, as they decided to fund a project in the 1970s,

80s and 90s, to investigate this curious phenomenon. A 'sensitive' named Ingo Swann successfully described accurately, and in detail, 43 out of 100 remote locations that were given to him to 'see', and another 32 in less detail. This was good enough for the Pentagon and they began to fund a program to find reliable psychic spies. Stargate was born. On the other side of the world, at the height of the Cold War, the Soviet Union was doing something very similar.

LEFT
The statue of the winged god Eros stands in London's Piccadilly Circus, although it was originally intended to be a statue of Anteros, Eros' brother

ABOVE The Pentagon, which houses the headquarters of the US Department of Defense, investigated remote viewing with the Stargate project

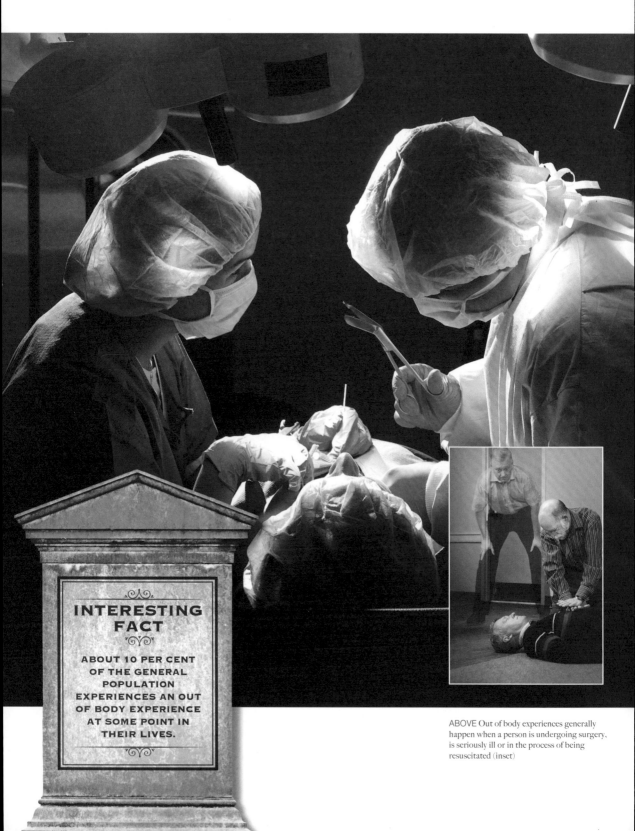

INTERESTING FACT

ABOUT 10 PER CENT OF THE GENERAL POPULATION EXPERIENCES AN OUT OF BODY EXPERIENCE AT SOME POINT IN THEIR LIVES.

ABOVE Out of body experiences generally happen when a person is undergoing surgery, is seriously ill or in the process of being resuscitated (inset)

OUT OF BODY EXPERIENCES

If there is one thing we know for sure about this life, it is that we are stuck with the body we have. As long as we are healthy, we should be glad that our body is working. Some psychics, however, experience sensations that allow them to leave their body behind.

An out of body experience varies from person to person, but it generally involves a feeling of floating away from your actual body. Usually people experiencing this unsettling phenomenon also look back down at their physical body, whether it's lying in a hospital bed, ll to do with the workings of the inner ear and how it connects with the brain. For those who have experienced it, however, it is said to bring a deep sense of fascination and understanding. Weirdly, they report that all their senses are still functioning; in fact they are working at a heightened level.

Some of the out of body experiences coincide with a medical crisis, a close shave with death. The person may be having a heart attack or be in surgery. Clinically, they may even die for a few minutes, if there is no recorded electrical activity in the brain. This is called a near death experience. A woman named Maria was visiting Seattle in the US when she had a heart attack. As the medical team worked on her body, her brain activity seemed to cease. Maria, however, was looking down on her body and the doctors, watching their actions and listening to their discussion. At one point, she left the room and saw an old tennis shoe on a ledge outside the third floor of the building.

When Maria 'came round', she told the doctors what had happened to her, including the details of the shoe. This could not be seen from the room where she was treated, but she begged someone to go and look for it.

Astonishingly, they found the shoe exactly where, and how, Maria had described it. Her consciousness had certainly remained alive, even if technically her brain had not.

TELEPATHY

When someone suggests you both go out to the very same place you were thinking of going, or expresses an opinion that you share, it's common to say, 'You read my mind!' Some extremely psychically gifted people, however, do actually seem to have this power.

This power is called telepathy and our knowledge of it dates back many centuries. At a basic level, telepathy involves mind reading – sensing another person's thoughts. At the next level, senders can influence and even restrict another person's physical movements using the power of their mind. Scarier still, they may claim to be able to influence their emotions and even to read their memories.

A well-known and extraordinary case of telepathy occurred back in Germany in the 19th century. Hans Berger was a bright boy who grew up to be an excellent student of mathematics at university. After graduation, Hans decided to take a break. He joined the army, enlisting in the cavalry. One day he was thrown from his horse during a training session and fell into the path of a team of horses charging towards him, pulling heavy cannons. Miraculously, the horses missed Hans' head by a fraction. At that exact moment, many miles away, Hans' sister was gripped by the knowledge that her brother was in terrible danger. She told her father of her fears and he was worried enough to send Hans a telegram, asking him if everything was alright. Somehow, Hans's intense fear as the horses charged towards him and he faced certain death had been transmitted to his sister. Telepathy often happens in times of heightened emotion like this. Hans was particularly close to his sister and again, telepathy works best when the sender and the receiver are emotionally bonded.

One excellent outcome of this episode was that Hans wanted to know more. He went back to university to study the activity of the brain, to understand what had happened to him. He found, of course, that telepathy is very difficult to test. Because the success of telepathy depends so much on the emotional state of both the sender and the receiver, it is difficult to replicate in a scientific setting. Hans did, however, discover much about the science of brain electricity, or brain waves, and he invented a machine to detect and record them. This never did prove the existence of telepathy, but it resulted in the EEG (electroencephalograph) machine, which is still used in medicine today.

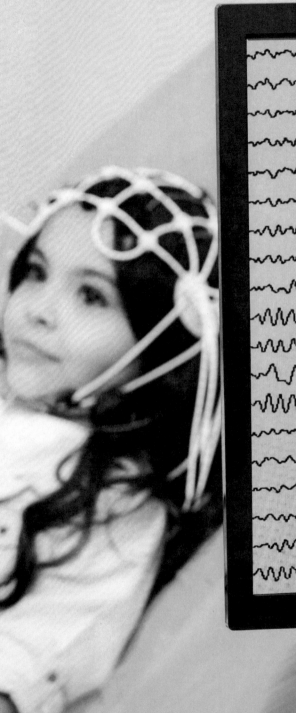

RIGHT The study of telepathy led to the development of the EEG machine, an essential tool in modern medicine

INTERESTING FACT

SOME PEOPLE BELIEVE THAT THE EXISTENCE OF DOPPELGÄNGERS IS PROOF THAT WE LIVE ALONGSIDE A PARALLEL UNIVERSE.

ABOVE Many people claim to have found their doppelgänger, but the chances of finding someone who exactly matches your facial characteristics is less than one in a trillion

INSET Goethe, whose tomb is shown here, was convinced he saw his doppelgänger

DOPPELGÄNGERS

Have you ever been in a public place and spotted someone who you were quite sure was someone you knew, only to find they were a stranger? It's an uncanny feeling, but not as unsettling as meeting somebody who actually looks exactly like you.

A surprising number of people around the world have met their 'doppelgänger', or double, also known as their twin stranger. These twins do look eerily similar, so much so that their family and friends may not be able to tell them apart. In the world of the paranormal, however, the doppelgänger is a far more sinister phenomenon.

We all think we are unique, so it's odd to meet someone who looks just like us. How much odder must it be, then, to meet your 'spirit double', your shadow self? This is the true meaning of a doppelgänger. The German word means literally 'double walker', and that describes the phenomenon perfectly. People claim to have seen the solid apparition of a living person whom they knew to be elsewhere at the time. That would be shocking enough, but for some psychically gifted few, the sight of their very own 'ghost' has been even more terrifying.

The idea that we all have a 'spirit double' goes back many centuries to the earliest civilisations and it is thought that an ancient pagan belief in a shadow self became the basis for the early Christian idea of a guardian angel. The appearance of a doppelgänger, however, is not usually

a welcome sign. It is seen as a sign of impending bad luck or death. The poet Shelley told his wife that he had seen his own ghost as he walked out on the terrace one day, and within two weeks he died by drowning in a boating accident, in 1822.

The German author and poet, Goethe had an experience that was just as inexplicable, if less fatal. While riding home from a visit to his girlfriend in Alsace, he saw his doppelgänger riding towards him. He was dressed in a grey and gold suit, in a style he never wore. Perplexed, Goethe kept his vision in mind, but carried on his way. Eight years later, riding back along the same road to visit the same girlfriend, he suddenly realised that he was indeed wearing a grey and gold suit exactly like the one in his vision and 'which I wore, not from choice, but by accident. However it may be with matters of this kind generally, this strange illusion in some measure calmed me'.

Could it be that poets have a more highly developed sense of intuition that strengthens their connection to the world of the spirit, that reality beyond the physical world in which most of us are content to live?

BILOCATION

Doppelgängers may have the power to astonish and alarm those who seem to meet themselves out in the world, but they appear only to the person having the vision. When this vision becomes visible to others, the phenomenon is known as bilocation.

In bilocation, the individual appears to be in two places at the exact same time. Inexplicable and extraordinary, these cases hint at powerful psychic powers. Both manifestations of the person seem totally present, living, breathing individuals, who can move and interact with their surroundings in a normal way. Perhaps unsurprisingly, many records of bilocation are of religious figures, people who appeared in a second location when they were badly needed to do good work. The Catholic Church accepts bilocation and considers it one of the core features required for conferring sainthood on an individual after their death. St Anthony of Padua was reported to have appeared in two different church services in Limoges, France, in 1226. He was clearly seen by dozens of churchgoers in both places.

In England in 1905, a Member of Parliament called Sir Frederick Carne Rasch was ill in bed with flu, unable to go out. An important debate was taking place in the House of Commons, however, and Sir Frederick's colleagues were surprised that evening to see him sitting on the backbenches, as they had been told he was unable to attend. Although he disappeared after a short while, several MPs were certain they had seen him – even though he had never left his bed. When confronted with this puzzle, Sir Frederick confirmed he had been very keen to attend the debate and seemed to accept that his willing it had made it happen.

LEFT
Vladimir Lenin was head of the government of Revolutionary Russia until his death in 1924

Another strange case occurred in the Soviet Union in 1923. Lenin was incapacitated in bed, after a series of strokes. A duty officer in the Kremlin was therefore surprised to see him in his office, searching urgently through his papers looking for something. Guards then saw Lenin strolling through the gardens, though without his customary walking stick. Had the Russian leader bilocated in his anxiety to complete some unfinished business? He was certainly not able to leave his bed, and a few months later he was dead.

ABOVE The Catholic Church considers bilocation as a qualifying miracle for sainthood

INTERESTING FACT

THE CATHOLIC CHURCH STATES THAT AT LEAST 18 OF ITS SAINTS HAVE BILOCATED, USUALLY WITH NUMEROUS WITNESSES.

CRYPTOZOOLOGY

The existence of strange phenomena is not confined to the sphere of humans. From every corner of the world come tales of paranormal creatures. The study of these mysterious animals is called cryptozoology.

Some cryptozoologists are scientists – men and women seeking to identify and explain these creatures, called cryptids, using the methods of their mainstream work. Others are fascinated in them as messengers from the unknown and seek to understand why they are here, what powers they may have and what we can learn from them. They are interested, too, in animal mythology, in how the stories of sightings and encounters with these beasts are passed from one generation to the next, as the legends around them grow. One thing we know for sure, these cryptids are skilled at keeping out of the way of humans. Despite all our technology, we have been unable to pin them down or even to prove their existence.

Britain is an island and the waters around its shores are excellent hiding places for mysterious creatures. In Falmouth Bay in Cornwall, for example, several witnesses have spotted a long-necked sea monster, called Morgawr, over the past 50 years. This evasive animal is not unlike the Loch Ness Monster – could they be related? Another has been recorded in the inland Lake Bala in North Wales, nicknamed Teggie, adding credence to this theory.

Off the coast of Benbecula, an island in the Outer Hebrides, people were cutting seaweed back in the 1830s when an apparition emerged from the waves. A boy threw a large stone at it and killed it, whereupon it washed up on the shore

– a mermaid! With the upper body of a young girl and the lower body and tail of a fish, the local residents were certainly convinced of what they saw, and gave it a formal funeral and burial on the island.

Back on land, the most common cryptids are peculiar, half-man-half-beast creatures, hairy hominids that lurk in our forests and secluded spaces. It seems that we can catch only fleeting glimpses of them, but these elusive mystery mammals have managed to keep their secrets from us for hundreds of years.

RIGHT and INSET The people of Benbecula, the small island off the west coast of Scotland, certainly believed they had seen a mermaid

BIGFOOT

Whether they stomp through snow or wade through swamps, there are many stories of mysterious ape-men defying our investigative powers. They emerge all around the world, but one of the most extraordinary is said to live in the Pacific Northwest of the US. Bigfoot.

This large primate walks upright on two legs, like a human. That is where the resemblance ends, however, for Bigfoot is covered in a shaggy coat of hair and has immensely powerful legs. In 1958, a man discovered a series of footprints at Bluff Creek in California. He made a cast of these mysterious prints and the story appeared in a local newspaper. Soon, people were calling the creature that had left these footprints Bigfoot and the name stuck. California is, however, thousands of kilometres from the Pacific Northwest. Up there, people began

reporting sightings of a large ape-like creature, 2–3 m (6–10 ft) tall, covered in dark brown or dark reddish hair. Some even claim to have got close enough to detect its strong, unpleasant smell. It leaves footprints up to 60 cm (2 ft) long and 20 cm (8 in) wide and seems mostly to come out at night. It is very strong and can run fast. It has been heard whistling, roaring and even screaming.

Bigfoot's other name is Sasquatch, which comes from a word used by the indigenous inhabitants of southeastern Canada, 'sasqets', meaning 'wild man'.

LEFT
Bigfoot is the best known of all the cryptids

Yet despite being the most widely documented of all the cryptids, Bigfoot still lurks on the fringes of our understanding. No one has captured definitive proof of its existence. In 1967, a man called Roger Patterson was out in the forest when he spotted a movement in the trees. Reaching for his film camera, he managed to capture almost a minute of footage. And what he recorded was quite incredible; a large, ape-like creature on two legs crossing a washed out creek and walking quickly back to the cover of the trees.

The scientific community does not believe Bigfoot is a real creature. They think he is merely a combination of folklore, misidentification and hoax. Those who have seen Bigfoot with their own eyes, however, would beg to differ.

ABOVE To come face-to-face with the Sasquatch would be no joke

INTERESTING FACT

SCIENTISTS ARGUE THAT FOR BIGFOOT TO SURVIVE THERE WOULD NEED TO BE A LARGE COMMUNITY OF ANIMALS FOR BREEDING.

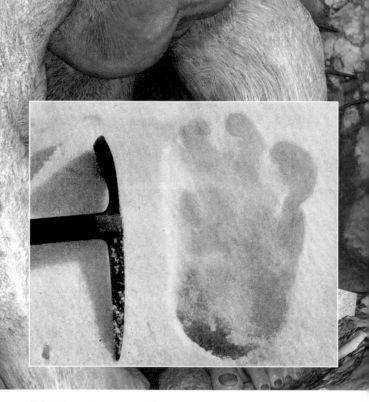

ABOVE This artist's impression of Yeti shows a muscular creature weighing 90–180 kg (200–400 lb)

INSET Eric Shipton found these tracks in the snow that look like they were made by a huge two-legged creature

YETI

Another mysterious ape-man in popular mythology is the Yeti. Like Bigfoot, this hairy humanoid has his own territory, this time Nepal and Tibet in the Himalayas, the vast Central Asian mountain range. Explorers and mountaineers have often reported sightings of this most imposing creature in the snowy wastes of this desolate landscape.

The story of a man-like beast in the Himalayas dates back centuries, to pre-Buddhist religion. The name Yeti comes from a word of the local Sherpa people, 'yeh-teh' meaning 'small, man-like animal'. The similarities with Bigfoot are obvious – both creatures walk upright leaving large footprints – and some think they belong to one species, a polar-bear-sized ape. This animal was native to southern Asia, but it has always been thought that it became extinct around 300,000 years ago. Could it have migrated to North America? Could it even have survived in its native Asia over all these centuries?

Back in 1951, an explorer called Eric Shipton certainly believed it could, because of what he saw with his own eyes. These were large footprints in the snow, not only long but also broad. Whenever they came to a narrow crevasse, or split, in the ground, these footprints acquired a new feature – distinct claw marks at the ends of the toe imprints. Something was clinging on to the snow extra hard, to cross these divides.

Fortunately, Shipton was able to take photographs of these footprints, and his discovery led to a flurry of scientific research into what this extraordinary creature could be.

Since then, many climbers have reported sightings of the creature, which is also sometimes known as the Abominable Snowman. They find tracks in the snow or, on rare occasions, catch a glimpse of the massive ape-human. In 1986, Reinhold Messner reported his extraordinary sighting of a yeti beside the Mekong River in Tibet: 'The creature towered menacingly, its face a grey shadow, its body a black outline.' He said that it was covered with hair and stood upright on two legs, while its arms were stocky and powerful.

BUNYIP

What is that lurking in the swamps, creeks and waterholes of
Australia? This mysterious cryptid is the bizarre-looking bunyip
and it has been terrifying the local people for generations.

The bunyip is a creature of Aboriginal
mythology. Its name comes from the
Wemba-Wemba language and means 'evil
spirit' or 'devil'. All across the continent,
people have reported seeing this
appalling creature, though descriptions
of its physical characteristics have varied.
Some say it has a dog-like face and dark
fur, others report a tail like that of a
horse, long flippers and walrus-like
tusks. All agree, however, that it is
predatory and terrifying. It has an
alarming taste for human flesh and lies
in wait in its watery lair, lashing out at
children and others who are foolish
enough to venture beyond the water's
edge. At night, it may even leave the
water and come in search of its
human prey.

The bunyip's sound is enough to chill the
senses, too, as it emits a low, hollow
boom, which becomes louder and more
insistent after dark.

The bunyip was first recorded in the
19th century by Westerners newly arrived
in Australia, but the Aboriginal people
were carving its likeness into the
landscape long before this, for they had
been plagued by this mysterious creature
for generations. They certainly believed
the creature had supernatural powers
and would do all they could to keep away
from it. They also believed, however,
that the bunyip was a punisher, a
creature sent to the world to bring
justice to those who do evil.

There is little hard evidence to help identify the bunyip. Large bones of a huge four-legged mammal found in a cave in Wellington in 1830 were thought to be those of a bunyip and in 1845 some strange fossils found near Geelong were again identified by a local man as belonging to the bunyip. One man then came forward to show the deep wounds on his chest that he claimed had been inflicted by the claws of this terrible animal.

Despite its elusive nature, the bunyip remains terrifying to the Australian people, who know better than to stray beyond the river bank or out into the creek, especially after dark.

INSET The bunyip remains an important part of their culture for many Australian people, not only for the Aboriginal people

RIGHT This image of the bunyip was printed on a postage stamp in 1994

LOCH NESS MONSTER

Out in the waters of a long, deep loch in the highlands of Scotland, there lurks a mysterious creature that has eluded identification for longer than anyone cares to remember.

For centuries, people have reported seeing a creature emerge fleetingly from the murky waters of Loch Ness. This enormous beast has a long neck, a smallish head and strong flippers. Nessie, as she is affectionately known, swims peacefully below the surface for most of the time, but once in a while she surfaces to survey the world. On these rare occasions she is sometimes spotted, but before anyone can reliably capture her image on film, she has slipped beneath the waves once more.

A fortunate few think they have spotted her, appearing briefly above the surface of this huge body of water. Some have taken photos, some have used sonar to record traces of her movements, others have used nothing more than the evidence of their own eyes. All agree that she is large and streamlined – and secretive. Could Nessie be a survivor from a prehistoric age, like the plesiosaurs of old? Or perhaps she is just an enormous eel-like creature or even a massive fish?

LEFT
This hoax photo of Nessie was one of the less-sophisticated attempts to prove her existence

The Loch Ness Monster was even used as propaganda in wartime. During World War II, an Italian newspaper owned by the country's dictator, Mussolini, claimed that a German bombing raid had scored a direct hit on Nessie, who had been finished off for good. Not so, claimed the locals. They were never going to swallow this assassination attempt on their favourite monster and sightings of Nessie continued resolutely. Of course, they were reported with delight by the British press.

The question of Nessie's diet has plagued investigators for decades. If she eats zooplankton, she would be able to catch them just by swimming about near the surface. Or perhaps Nessie is nocturnal and she has only emerged to eat fish during the day very rarely down the years, when she had no other choice but to show herself?

ABOVE If the Loch Ness monster is real, it could look like an ancient plesiosaur

INTERESTING FACT

IF NESSIE EATS FISH, SHE MUST LIVE IN THE TOP 4–5 M (13–16 FT) OF WATER TO BE ABLE TO SEE THEM, UNLESS SHE HAS ANOTHER WAY TO DETECT THEM.

INTERESTING FACT

THE BEAST OF EXMOOR HAS BEEN KNOWN TO JUMP FENCES 1.8 M (6 FT) HIGH.

ABOVE Parts of Exmoor National Park are only accessible on foot or by rough track – the ideal place for a large predator to hide

INSET Does a terrifying creature like this black panther roam the wilds of Exmoor?

BEAST OF EXMOOR

There are few truly wild places left in Britain, but Exmoor is certainly one of them, a desolate stretch of moorland that connects the two counties of Devon and Somerset in the west of England. Out here, ever since the 1970s, people have been reporting sightings of a large, dark beast.

The official version is that the Beast of Exmoor does not exist, but this phantom creature has been reported many, many times over the years. Can an imaginary beast be responsible for the killing of more than 100 sheep in a series of frenzied attacks over the course of one month? This is what happened to one farmer in the 1970s. He walked out into his fields to find all his animals with their throats viciously slashed open.

Sightings of this ferocious predator have continued since then and the local farmers know to be very, very wary of it. They can tell when their animals are afraid, which they often are. Back in the 1980s, the authorities decided something must be done. They sent in a group of sharpshooters from the Royal Marines, no less, to finally bring down the beast. Some reported seeing it, but despite their best efforts no shots were fired.

What could this beast possibly be? People have described a large animal with a long, curling tail with a rounded end. It walks, or slinks, rather like a cat, but is significantly bigger than a domestic cat. Whatever it is, it needs to eat, and to eat it must kill. It may do most of its hunting at night, but sometimes it breaks cover during daylight hours.

Occasionally it appears close enough to the road so that drivers think they catch a fleeting glimpse of it as they speed along. Most accounts describe a big cat rather like a panther or a puma, up to 2.4 m (8 ft) long and extremely agile. These cats are not native to Britain, so if there is a beast like this roaming the west country, it is a mystery how it ever came to be there.

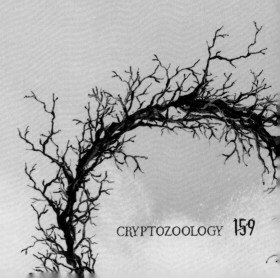

MOTHMAN

We travel next to West Virginia in the US, in search of one of the
weirdest creatures ever to emerge in the world of cryptozoology.
This is a creature that, in the late 1960s, was linked to a host of
parapsychological events in the area where it was seen.

Its name was Mothman and it appeared as
a winged, man-sized being, with large,
reflective red eyes and extraordinary
moth-like wings. In the Charleston and
Point Pleasant areas of West Virginia, in
the late autumn of 1966, the first
eyewitness account came in of a sighting of
this bizarre creature. Five men at the local
cemetery, digging a grave for a burial, saw
a mysterious 'brown human being' lift off
from some nearby trees and fly above
their heads. This was no bird, but how
could it possibly be a winged man?

Over the next few days, more accounts
began to come through of this ominous,
air-borne apparition. Two young married
couples were driving by an old World
War II Ordnance Works when they saw
two red lights in the shadows. Pulling
over, they realised they were the shining
eyes of a huge animal, 'shaped like a man,
but bigger ... with big wings folded
against its back'. It proceeded to chase
them as they drove away at top speed. On
that same night, in the same area, Newell
Partridge was at home when he heard his
dog Bandit howling loudly at something
outside. Going out to investigate, he was
shocked to see two large red eyes glowing
from the family barn. He returned to the
house and secured the doors, but in the
morning there was no sign of Bandit. All

Newell could see were the tracks of his dog going round and round in a circle outside, as if he had been barking at something above him, in the air. The dog was never seen again.

The townspeople began to panic. They combed the area, but only ever saw the Mothman flying overhead, often alongside their cars as they sped away to get clear of it. Over the months that followed, sightings grew scarcer, but there were enough to keep people wary. What was the meaning of this appalling series of events? Was it a sign of an impending tragedy that was about to afflict their area? Then, in December 1967, the Mothman was spotted several times sitting on the top of a local bridge, the Silver Bridge over the Ohio River. On the evening of the 15th December, the Silver Bridge suddenly collapsed, sending 46 cars plunging into the river. Many people died in this atrocity, but an investigation revealed that the bridge had failed structurally at one single, small point in a suspension chain – where the Mothman had been seen perching.

†+‡+†

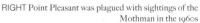

RIGHT Point Pleasant was plagued with sightings of the Mothman in the 1960s

OWLMAN OF MAWNAN

The sleepy Cornish village of Mawnan Smith nestles on the estuary of the River Helford, with a handful of houses and a picturesque church. This idyllic spot has been the scene of some terrifying events.

There are curious parallels between the stories of the Owlman of Mawnan and the Mothman of West Virginia. Back in 1976, two young girls were on holiday in the area when they saw what they later described as a 'bird man' hovering over the tower of Mawnan church. Scared out of their wits, they ran to the local police station, where they were asked to draw what they had seen. Both girls, in separate rooms, drew pictures of a creature about 1.8 m (6 ft) tall and covered in feathers, its huge wings outstretched to at least 3 m (10 ft). Most terrifying of all, it screeched loudly into the skies and its large red eyes glowed a fiery red.

Not long after this, more witnesses spotted the Owlman standing on the branch of a tall pine tree, looming over them. At first they thought it was a local prankster in costume, but when it took off and flew away into the night they knew this was no joke. Since then, there have been numerous sightings of strange red lights and hissing sounds near the church. Some who have had a closer look have reported huge claws emanating from the Owlman's vast wings.

What is going on here? Certainly the church at Mawnan stands at the centre of a prehistoric earthwork that could be a burial and some researchers have

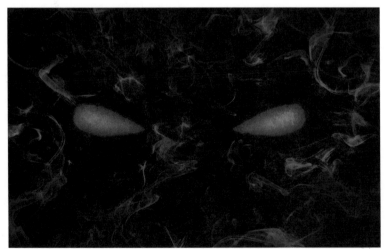

LEFT
All reports of the Owlman feature its slanting red eyes glowing out of the darkness

detected a ley line passing through the site. Ley lines are alignments of places of ancient religious and spiritual significance and are said to be places of great psychic energy. Could this energy have generated this terrible cryptoid? Certainly, the Owlman is seen as a malevolent entity and some have suggested he is the manifestation of an ancient owl-god, worshipped thousands of years ago by the Phoenicians, who sacrificed children as offerings to please him. We know that the Phoenicians sailed to Cornwall to trade. Whatever, or whoever, it is, the people of Mawnan know not to venture into their churchyard at night.

†✝‡✝†

ABOVE The eagle owl is a magnificent creature of awesome power – could people have mistaken the sinister Owlman for this elegant bird?

INTERESTING FACT

LEY LINES ARE BELIEVED TO CONNECT SACRED PLACES, SUCH AS STONEHENGE AND THE GREAT PYRAMIDS, WITH LINES OF MAGNETIC ENERGY.

ABOVE Would you go out of your way to find a ghost in a spooky place at night?

GHOST HUNTING

The idea of seeing a ghost is thrilling for some people, terrifying for others. It is certainly true that ghost hunting has become big business. You can go on night-time tours of castles and stately homes, inns and graveyards, in search of ghouls and other evidence of the paranormal.

There are even television shows devoted to the pursuit of ghosts, too, where huge crews invade these locations to capture 'the unseen' for our entertainment. It is hard to think of a scenario where any spirits from the 'other side' are less likely to make an appearance, yet millions of people enjoy the programmes. We just cannot shake off our fascination with the mysterious, with the possibility of realms of existence beyond the grave.

For those who are serious about the pursuit of paranormal knowledge, however, these mass-market events are not the key to success. Almost everyone who experiences an encounter with a spirit does so when they are alone. This makes it more frightening, possibly, but also more difficult to assess objectively. In the 19th century, when reports of ghost sightings began to escalate and when science began to develop rapidly as a serious field of study, the two phenomena came together. Men of a scientific turn of mind, and it was almost exclusively men rather than women, decided to try to investigate ghosts and the paranormal scientifically.

All investigations require equipment. At first, the equipment of professional ghost hunters was quite basic and so it remained until the late 20th century.

One of the most famous early ghost hunters was Harry Price, who worked in the 1920s and 30s. His most famous case was Borley Rectory, where he moved in and set up a 'laboratory' to record what was happening. His equipment included a portable telephone, a telescope, cameras, a tape measure, felt overshoes to make his feet silent, a torch and some electromagnetic lighting. Over many years he documented movements, noises and apparitions at Borley, but despite this pseudo-scientific approach he still had a strong sense of the theatrical. He made live broadcasts from haunted houses for the BBC, seven decades before the ghost-hunting shows we know and love today. After his death, much of his work was discredited and it took the invention of more sophisticated technology for the art of ghost hunting to move on.

RIGHT and INSET Ghost hunting programmes that stake out apparently haunted houses have become popular television viewing

SOCIETIES FOR PSYCHICAL RESEARCH

The Victorians loved Societies – official bodies of more or less qualified men who gathered together to discuss and advance their knowledge in the subjects in which they shared an interest. Unsurprisingly, the British Society for Psychical Research was founded in these times, in 1882.

As interest in the afterlife and the paranormal grew rapidly through the 19th century, more people took this as an opportunity to make money. Individuals longing to connect with their departed loved ones could easily be parted with their cash, on the promise of a séance at which they could meet again. The unscrupulous exploited these vulnerable people and there was a big increase in the number of fake mediums and other spiritual guides. The SPR was founded to try to establish the difference between these fakes and the genuine psychics who appeared to be able to reach out to the 'other side', whether through séances, automatic writing, telepathy or clairvoyance of some kind. They would use the best scientific methods available to them to achieve this. Their work established a new field of study, called parapsychology.

The SPR was a respected body of intellectual gentlemen. Early members included high profile figures such as Sir Arthur Conan Doyle, Arthur Balfour, Sigmund Freud and Carl Jung. Inspired by scientific ideals, they were determined not to be misled by tricks, illusions and wishful thinking, quickly learning to spot fake mediums after sitting through endless false séances.

The foundation of their work was the collection of data. Various committees studied numerous instances of telepathy, hypnotism and clairvoyance, as well as hauntings and apparitions. In 1886, they published *Phantasms of the Living*, with analysis of more than 700 personal experiences of apparitions.

LEFT
Sigmund Freud with his mother, in 1925

The SPR also worked closely with similar bodies in other countries, including the American Society for Psychical Research in the United States.

The founding fathers of the SPR were scholars of classics and philosophy and after their deaths a number of mediums, working independently, began to receive messages through automatic writing. They understood almost nothing of the writings they received, but the SPR researchers investigating them, who themselves had knowledge of classical and philosophical texts, were astonished when they began to put them together. A single organising intelligence appeared to be behind the messages. This, they believed, was their deceased colleagues attempting to provide proof of their survival from the 'other side'.

ABOVE Edmund Gurney was a prominent English parapsychologist in the late 1800s, who contributed to *Phantasms of the Living*

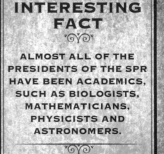

INTERESTING FACT

ALMOST ALL OF THE PRESIDENTS OF THE SPR HAVE BEEN ACADEMICS, SUCH AS BIOLOGISTS, MATHEMATICIANS, PHYSICISTS AND ASTRONOMERS.

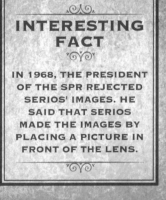

ABOVE Today, technology can produce 'paranormal' illusions all too easily

INSET Ted Serios produced extraordinary 'thoughtographs'. He was described by some as psychopathic and sociopathic

PHOTOGRAPHY

When we want to capture an image, we simply click the camera or press a button on our phones. We take millions of images, but can this technology work on visitors from the spirit world? The early ghost hunters believed it could and some of them produced the images to prove it.

In these days of everyday image manipulation, it can be difficult to remember that in the early days of photography, trickery would have been a complicated business. On the other hand, the simplicity of the processes could also lead to some basic technical errors, producing strange results that could be misinterpreted as ghostly apparitions. So accidental double exposures on the same photographic plate or film negative could produce faint images of otherworldly faces or objects in the photograph. This did not stop unscrupulous hoaxers from offering spirit photography to the gullible, but as investigators exposed them, the public became more aware of the tricks that could be done and the amount of deception began to decline.

The case of Ted Serios was a very curious one. Ted worked as a porter in a Chicago hotel in the 1960s, but his main interest was in 'thoughtography'. This extraordinary phenomenon involved a person being able to imprint a photographic image onto chemical film – using the power of thought alone. No camera was needed.

Ted discovered that he had the power to do this and he did indeed produce thousands of images of people and places. Sceptics and investigators imposed strictly controlled environments on him, but still the images came. How could this be? One of the most remarkable was of the home of the parapsychologist called Eisenbud who was investigating him. This was a ranch just outside Denver, but when the image was developed Eisenbud was astonished to see an image of his house without the white shutters that he had added a few years earlier. This was a 'thoughtograph' of his home from the past.

Today, modern photographic techniques are used in paranormal investigations. Digital cameras are avoided, for obvious reasons, so regular 35 mm cameras, sometimes with heat-sensitive infrared film, are set up instead. Any sudden change in conditions will trigger them to take a photograph.

MODERN GHOST HUNTING

Anyone wanting to investigate ghosts today needs some serious kit. This most mysterious of worlds requires sophisticated equipment to capture whatever is trying to reach us from the realms of the paranormal.

Ghost hunters will always carry a stills camera and a video camera, with infrared devices fitted to these to allow pictures to be recorded in the dark, when experience suggests apparitions are most likely. A Geiger counter can record changes in radiation levels in the atmosphere and a negative ion counter will catch changes in the volume of negative ions in the air, both of which seem to be features of paranormal manifestations.

Perhaps the most important weapon in the investigator's arsenal, however, is the electromagnetic field (EMF) meter. This measures changes in the electromagnetic field in any location. Many electrical appliances generate their own EMFs, so these must first be measured so that any variances due to the otherwise inexplicable can be recorded accurately. Thunderstorms produce EMFs too, but then again stormy nights are surely one of the favourite roaming times for ghosts as well?

Do the dead speak to us when they return from the 'other side'? Few people have actually heard a ghost speak, but investigators often set up equipment to catch any sounds they make that the living human ear cannot detect.

Electronic voice phenomena (EVP) has become increasingly sophisticated, as digital devices scan a wide range of sound frequencies. Picking up spirit voices embedded in the atmosphere may sound strange, but both photography and X-ray were once thought to be paranormal. If we have learned one thing from history, it is that things that once scared us have often later been explained by science and have become an accepted part of our everyday world, so who knows?

All the measurements from an investigation are collected to produce a picture of what is going on. A repeated pattern of unusual results, or an extreme level of results, will ring alarm bells.

INSET EMF meters are an essential tool for the modern ghost hunter

RIGHT This image was taken using a thermal imaging camera, a tool for detecting changes in infrared radiation – a sign that paranormal activity is taking place

25.3 °C

7.2

GOING ON A GHOST HUNT

Seasoned ghost hunters are not afraid. They are curious. They know that if you let your imagination run away with you, you can let fear of the unknown take over, resulting in panic – and most likely in an unsuccessful session.

Many would say they are ghost observers rather than hunters, that these figures from beyond the grave do not deserve to be hunted. They once lived on Earth as we do, with the same cares and joys that we have, but for whatever reason they have been unable to find peace after death. We should treat them with respect, while we try to understand what they are trying to tell us.

Setting out in search of ghosts, we should be aware of what we are getting into. The vast majority of ghostly experiences are no such thing.

Draughts, rattling plumbing, creaky doors and the wind can explain all manner of sensations. Our state of mind can predispose us to think we are experiencing something strange, too – if we are tense and anxious, we may interpret anything as creepy. On the other hand, perhaps we should have an open mind as well.

The paranormal may not be scientifically proven, but many aspects of paranormal and psychic activity cannot be disproved, either. Sometimes, all we need is the evidence of our own senses.

LEFT
Ghost hunters keep an open mind – and their cameras at the ready

ABOVE Stories of ghosts and the paranormal suggest that something more may await us beyond the grave

A chill in one corner of a room, an unusual smell, fleeting glimpses of lights or misty shadows, footsteps coming from and going to nowhere or the brush of a dress against the leg; all these have convinced individuals that they were not quite alone.

There are unfathomable examples of clairvoyance from all around the world. Mediums have related details of loved ones who have died that it seems they could not possibly have known. Open spaces, from the oceans to the moors, have been the scenes of unsettling, if not terrifying experiences for some and in all corners of the world's homes, those intimate spaces where people have lived and died, have manifested traces of spirits who have felt unable to leave their most precious places behind.

✝✝✝✝

INDEX

PICTURE CREDITS

Cover: see imprint page.

Inside: background and incidental images by iStock/Getty.

All feature images by Shutterstock except:

Alamy Stock Photo: Alan Gallery: p. 82; Art Collection 2: p. 89 (inset);
Aurora Photos: p. 58; Chronicle: p. 11; Classic Image : p. 83;
Roger Cracknell 28/Mexico: p. 59 (inset); Toby de Silva: p. 13; Dinodia Photos: p. 38; Everett Collection
Inc: p. 12; GL Archive: p. 48 (inset); Rik Hamilton: p. 10;
Robert Harding: p. 36; Adrian-Catalin Lazar: p. 28; Anne Lewis: p. 59; Phil Rees: p. 14;
Science History Images: p. 80; Alex Segre: p. 48; Alexey Senin: p. 44;
Parinya Suwanitch: p. 30; Marc Zakian: p. 34.

Getty Images: Allan Baxter: p. 32; Joanna Cepuchowicz/EyeEm: p. 65;
DeAgostini: p. 29 (inset); Patrick Doherty: p. 31; Aaron Vincent Elkaim: p. 52;
Historica Graphica Collection/Heritage Images: p. 47;
Thurston Hopkins/Picture Post: p. 14 (inset); JTB Photo/UIG: p. 50;
Jason Maehl: p. 44 (inset); Pete Turner: p. 46;
Wikimedia Commons: p. 68 (inset), p. 117, p. 167; E. W. Allen: p. 107 (inset);
Tim Bertelink: p. 161; Beyond my Ken: p. 19; Bidgee: p. 17 (inset);
Jule Eisenbud: p. 168 (inset); Holger Ellgaard: p. 78; Ian Freeman: p. 76;
Arnold Genthe: p. 127; Geographer: p. 61; Maad Dog 97: p. 79; Ad Meskens: p. 156; Karl-Heinz
Meurer: p. 144 (inset); Rodolpho Hugo Mikulasch: 120, 121;
Ministry of Information Photo Division Photographer: p. 118; Mostlymade: p. 160; National Media
Museum: p. 119; Neil Rickards: p. 77 (inset); Elisa Rolle: p. 74; Rwendland: p. 20-21; Saychinquai: p. 53;
Eric Shipton/Gardner Soule: p. 152 (inset); Spacemountainmike: p. 74 (inset); Wellcome Images: p. 55;
Jim Winstead: p. 94; Stefan Wolmarans: p. 77; ullstein bild Dtl.: p. 126.